CHANCE OF A LIFETIME

Best Wishes,

Ann Chance.

Written by
Ann Chance

First Published in Great Britain in 2006 by Tucann Books
Text © Ann Chance All rights reserved
Design © TUCANN*design&print*
Reprinted 2007

ISBN 10: 1 873257 71 6
ISBN 13: 9781873257715

Produced by: TUCANN*design&print*, 19 High Street, Heighington Lincoln LN4 1RG
Tel & Fax: 01522 790009
www.tucann.co.uk

CONTENTS

FOREWORD

You might have heard Ann Chance as a Professional after dinner speaker and entertainer.

This book is to let you know, that there is much more to this lady than just one or two exploits.

As you read on, you will see that Ann is a very normal human being and that her life, like so many of us, has had its ups and downs.

We have published this book because Ann has a knack of making the most of given situations by taking A. Chance.

We hope that her stories will inspire others to "Go for your dreams" and perhaps like Ann discover that so much more can be gained from life by helping other people to achieve their dreams and ambitions.

Ann was born in 1938 to working class parents in Balham, known as "Gateway to the south".

Her parents divorced and remarried, (not to each other), very common today, but not then.

She claims she was not academic but still managed to pass her 11 plus exam. She excelled at sport and her greatest pride was to play Korfball for her country. Whatever she did, she did it well.

At the age of 21, Ann married into a family of Hardware Merchants and together with her husband worked to develop the businesses, culminating in her becoming the first ever Lady President of the Associated Trade Organisation.

Her sporting activities had to take a back seat after becoming a mother of two sons.

Not only was she now helping with the businesses, looking after two boys but finding the time to teach herself to play the guitar, clarinet, ukulele, alto saxophone, plus ordinary things like comb and paper.

Through her involvement with the Rotary club, she also, at this time, took part in fund raising concerts, where at one time had the honour to share a dressing room with Cardew Robinson.

The businesses expanded until finally in 1987 they were all sold. Ann and her husband divorced, leading her to look for new challenges. It was not long before her famous exploits began.

As far as health is concerned Ann laughs and claims to be a bionic woman. She has had many "bits" taken away and other "bits" replaced.

Not only has she been a migraine sufferer since the age of 11, but had her tonsils removed at 38, a partial hysterectomy at 42, breast cancer at 57 a heart attack at 67 and now in 2006 one of her knees had to be replaced as it had worn out, but she still goes on and will not admit defeat.

Ann says, "I am a mum and a Granny and whilst I will admit to being 68, I will not submit…YET". "No matter what knocks you receive throughout your life, providing you have the courage and conviction, tinged with a bit of stupidity you will probably be able to achieve most things".

So her advice to anyone approaching mid-life crisis is to reach for your dreams and – GO FOR IT.

We hope you will enjoy this book.

Editor.
Tucann Books.

INTRODUCTION BY WAY OF
"UVER FINGS WOT I 'AVE DUN"

Despite growing up in Balham, I passed my eleven plus exam and went to the Rosa Bassett School for young ladies. When I first went there it was known as Streatham Grammar. The lady who founded the school was Miss Rosa Bassett and after she had been dead for two hundred years, the Governors, in their wisdom could think of no better way to commemorate her memory than to change the name of the school from Streatham Grammar to Rosa Bassett School for young ladies. When you are young and live in Balham and you are asked out on a date, the boyfriend asks you, "Wot school do you go oo darlin'?" When the reply is, "Well actually, I attend Rosa Bassett School for young ladies". I can assure you, he very quickly disappears. If I could have said, "Cor, mate I go to Streatham Grammar". I think I could have been onto a certainty.

Our school motto, translated from the Latin meant, Hold fast to that which is good. As there were two boys' schools around the corner from ours, I can assure you that I did my level best to live up to the school motto as often as I could.

I never did understand how I had managed to get to a Grammar school. My Mother always told me that I would never make anything of my life and that I was no where near as clever as my Father or my Sister.

I didn't enjoy my time at the senior School the subjects were too academic for me, at the time to grasp. However I was very good at Gymnastics, Acrobatics and Sport. Too many subjects in my opinion were on the syllabus. I had to study, English, French, German, Latin and Greek. History, Geography, Mathematics, Algebra, Geometry, Logarithms, Science, Physics, Chemistry, Cooking, Sewing, Economics and Social Studies. Then there was Music, Singing and Dancing, Gymnastics and Sport. Netball, Tennis and Hockey. There was no time to enjoy myself at all.

As I have already stated I was good at sport and gymnastics.

At the age of thirteen I learnt to play Korfball on Tooting Bec Common. Korfball is a Dutch Game, which was brought over to England in 1942. This is a winter sport played Sunday mornings outdoors on grass about the size of a football pitch. The goal post is an eleven foot three inch pole stuck in the ground with a large metal spike and at the top is a solid double open ended basket.

The pitch is divided into three equal sections, known as Attack, Centre and Defence. Each team consists of six boys and six girls. The girls mark the girls and the boys mark the boys. Shame really. It could be quite fun if these rules were not adhered to. There was a good side to this rule, the girls although not allowed to tackle the boys often did, if the Referee was not looking. If he was, and caught us out, we girls would usually apologise and say, "I'm sorry Ref I thought it was a girl". He never believed us and awarded a penalty. By the age of eighteen I had the highest goal average in the country and was chosen to play for England twice.

There is a Federation of International Korfball, affectionately known as F.I.K.

Our team travelled to Holland on more than one occasion to play the Nationals at their own game. I thought I was a good player up to this point. In Holland I was playing against ladies much older than myself and I conceitedly thought I would run rings around them. I was very wrong, they left me standing. Being their National game the players had grown up with Korfball and put me in my place.

Years later, my niece who lives in Mitcham, phoned me and said that she was being taught how to play Korfball at her school. The game had been taken into the gym, fewer players and a lower goal post. As I had been an England player, would I please go to support her in a match to be held at Epsom College? What an honour. How could I refuse?

I ran up and down the sidelines during the match, telling her what to do and how to do it and screaming things like, NO, NOT LIKE THAT, LOOK BEHIND YOU, RUN, SHOOT, plus anything else that came to mind. At half time the referee, who was the Gym teacher came and spoke to me and said, "I have a feeling that you know something about this game". "Your niece has told me that you played for England". I smiled with pride and puffed out my chest. He then told me that both his Mother and Father had also played for England. I said, "Your Mum isn't Joyce and your Dad Martin?" He replied, "Yes". I was gob smacked and I replied, "You're not the little boy who used to be in a carrycot on the sidelines every Sunday morning?" He confirmed that yes, this was him. What a nice thought that now he had grown up and was teaching my niece how to play the sport. It's a small world isn't it?

As my Korfball club at the time was quite small, funds became a problem. Every year we would form an entertainments committee and write and produce a show to put on at the local assembly rooms.

At one of the script writing meetings a couple of the lads said, "If we could get a Soho Stripper to perform at one of our shows, just look at the money we could earn". I didn't like the way they were looking at me. After a lot of begging and cajoling, at the age of eighteen I became a stripper.

There was no way I was going to do the full Monty. I had roughly three months in which to rehearse and prepare for this feat.

I firstly took myself to a strip joint to watch how it was done. Strippers in those days were different to today; they started with clothes on and

9

then slowly and tantalizingly took the items off one at a time. Not so today, they start out with little or nothing on and wrap themselves around a pole. It's not the same is it? But then; I'm a woman and probably see things differently to men.

I then purchased a record of the original stripper music. Oh boy; what a great piece of music. You can't help but get your clothes off when you play that. A small note here, if your love life needs a lift, buy this record, it's a hell of a lot cheaper than Viagra and a lot more fun.

The clothing was the next hurdle. I knew that a suspender belt and stockings would be the order of the night. In my day, the part of a woman's body that men seemed to find attractive was the gap between the top of the stockings and the knickers, plus being able to twang the suspenders.

I then purchased a flesh coloured body stocking and a black pair of knickers with a bell and flowers on the front. The next items were a black bra' with coloured polka dots, onto which I sowed tassels in an appropriate place.

I tried for nearly three weeks to get them going round without success. I think professionals must use batteries.

Black fish net stockings were needed next.

I would be wearing a three quarter length dress with frills at the hem, a fur stole, long white gloves, a full length wig, false eyelashes and very heavy make up as I didn't wish to be recognised.

No one in my club, other than the committee was to know who the stripper was.

One of our local Electricians put blue lighting on the stage to create the right atmosphere.

On the day of the performance I was so nervous I was running a high temperature. I felt that in the true tradition of a performer, "The Show must go on".

The compere made his announcement; "Ladies and Gentlemen, now for your delectation and delight, please welcome, at great expense to our club, the world famous Soho Stripper".

The music started and the curtains parted slowly and tentatively I stuck a leg out. This was immediately greeted with shouts of, "Don't muck about, get 'em off". Of course I ignored these bestial remarks and continued at my rehearsed level.

Sitting on the stage were seven boys from our club, with their backs to the audience watching my every move. This was part of the act.

I firstly began to roll the long sleeved gloves down my arm and threw them at the audience. Unfortunately they landed around the neck of the Mayor sitting in the front row. He was O.K. but his wife looked a little disturbed.

I reached the point where the only things I was still wearing were Bra' and knickers.

I turned my back to the audience to pretend to undo the hooks, this was where the boys were supposed to rush at me and pretend to strip me naked. They had become so engrossed at what was happening, they never moved. I very nearly panicked at this point as I was getting a lot of offers of help from the audience.

I worked my way along the line of boys and kicked them in turn saying, "Move you swine, before I get arrested. Suddenly they stood up and rushed at me with such energy I screamed in terror as I wasn't sure what they were going to do next.

The curtains were hurriedly pulled and a mock fight took place back stage. On the fire hydrant there was an identical bra and pants which the boys took, they then ran through the half open curtains down into the audience waiving said articles over their heads. They were even shouting and saying things like, "Get off I got them first and ooh, they're still warm". I then appeared on stage with a full length dressing gown wrapped very tightly around me trying to look embarrassed as if I had no clothes on.

I was eighteen when all this took place and I am now sixty eight. I mention this because our club earned over four hundred pounds that night. Just think what I could be earning today. I'm sure I could still perform because I have the same equipment, but there's a bit more of it now and it's not in the same place as it used to be.

Most of the girls in my club had still not realised that I was the Soho stripper. One day in the changing rooms after a game of Korfball, some of the girls were chatting and saying how terrific that stripper was at the show. I thought they knew and were winding me up. They asked me what I thought of her and true to form I went along with what I thought was their joke and I said, "Personally I thought she was tremendous". So I told them that it had been me but they would not believe this.

During that year I was President of the club and at the annual Dinner and Dance, I decided to wear the same outfit that I had performed the striptease in. The girl's faces were a picture and at long last they were now convinced that it had been me.

During my time at school I never seemed able to pass an exam, I did however, gain a very high level distinction mark in Salad Preparation. You see I was good at something. At least you will know who to contact if you hold a Dinner Party and need a salad. I hold a certificate that says I am good at it.

I also acquired another high level distinction mark, this time, in French Aural. I went into the examination room and sat down at the table, in front of the teacher. On the wall behind her she had pinned up a picture. I would now like to paint this for you to add to the atmosphere.

There was a clear blue sky dotted with fluffy white clouds. There was a grass and tree covered mountain gently sloping down to a lake of a beautiful light blue in colour. On this lake was a wooden rowing boat and in the boat was a man with a fishing rod, would you believe, fishing. There was a plush green grassy bank upon which was a wooden shed. Seated next to the shed was a little dog, looking out on to the lake at the man in the fishing boat...... fishing? My French examiner asked me in French, which I am not able to do you'll be pleased to know. "Did I think that the dog sitting on the green grassy bank next to the wooden shed, looking out onto the lake below the mountain and clear blue sky with fluffy white clouds at the man in the wooden fishing boat with a fishing rod, fishing, was it possible that this was his dog?" What would you say if anyone asked you such a stupid question in your own language? I have to be honest I hadn't really understood the entire question and I knew I had two choices for an answer. I chose, "Oui, peut-etre. You probably all know that this means, Yes, perhaps. My French examiner gave me a high level distinction mark and told me that I had a tremendous command of the French language. I was already beginning to learn that if you pretend that you have something between your ears, other than wax, all things could be possible.

As I loved sport and was good at it, I was made Captain of the Netball Team, Tennis, Hockey and Swimming. At the time I did not have my bronze medal for life saving and I felt that as Captain this should be obligatory. One of my friends said she would be my partner and offered to drown for me. On arrival at the designated swimming pool, my friend dived in and swam to the deep end of the pool and proceeded to pretend to drown. I was then made to put on a pair of pyjamas, dive in and swim to the deep end to affect the rescue. On reaching the victim I trod water and removed the pyjama trousers. I subdued her struggles and held onto her tightly, whilst putting the trousers round her neck to act as a floatation collar. Very strange you might think but absolutely true. Let me paint another picture. It's a lovely sunny Sunday afternoon and you are walking the dog along the local canal towpath and you hear someone screaming for help. Upon locating them, drowning, all you need to say is, "Could you wait here a minute whilst I run home and fetch my pyjamas?"

Occasionally, I was allowed to take the Gymnastics class, whilst leading up to the very many exhibitions which my team gave to other schools and Hospitals. I always wanted more acrobatics and Gymnastics than was able to be taught during the school term time, so I illegally joined a boys' Gymnastic class out of school hours. The reason it was illegal for girls was due to the fact that we would be executing vaults that would put a strain on the parts of a woman's' body that might later in life bear children. This school was visited regularly by inspectors to make sure that the rules were being adhered to and that the class was run safely. When I knew that their visit was coming I would hide inside the box whilst the boys demonstrated their tremendous gymnastic ability by leaping over the box one at a time. One would be on the springboard, one would be in the air and one would be landing. As you can imagine the timing was critical. I was watching this performance through the hand holds of the box. Something got a hold of me at one point and as one of the boys took off from the springboard, I poked my hand through the hole. His first reaction was to cough in surprise and to then fall face down onto the top of the box. The speed, with which the others were following, made the vault impossible and they all piled on top of each other. The inspector said that he thought they were a pleasant bunch of boys but their gymnastics need a bit of polish. I thought I'd better leave, before I was beaten to a pulp.

On leaving school at sixteen and a half without any worthwhile qualifications, I was at a loss to decide what to do with my life. My Dad suggested that I apply for a job in Harrods and much to my surprise, I was accepted. I really think that the only reason they took me on was because when they inquired as to which school I had attended, I said, "Rosa Bassett

School for young Ladies. It wasn't long before I realised that I had been born and bred in Balham and that my vocabulary was slightly different to the other staff. I dropped my 'H's' and could not pronounce a double 'T'. I decided to have some private elocution lesson to put this matter right. This made me feel as if I was fitting in better. Clothing was a problem as I could not afford good quality and most of my outfits were darned. If I did not have a black skirt, which was the uniform, I would have to dye one of my other skirts to meet the managements' requirements. With time, I improved and gradually began to feel more at home in this very strange lucrative environment. I began to show a flair for in store window dressing and was allowed to do just that, which again made me realise that there are a few more things that I can do.

One day an Italian family came into our department and asked the buyer for the interpreter. Unfortunately the store only had one and he was engaged elsewhere. The buyer came over to me and said, "Ann do you speak Italian?" to which I replied, "Si". With a big sigh of relief she said, "Well please go and help this Italian family". I didn't like to tell her that was the only word I knew. I might be able to order Spaghetti Bolognaise or duo Cocoa Cola por favori. Apart from those two phrases that was about it. You know when you have opened your mouth and put both feet right in it don't you? But, not downhearted I approached this family. They consisted of Mum and Dad, Nan and Granddad, Aunty and Uncle, three small boys and two small girls. All the adults were dressed in the traditional long black clothing. They quite frightened me as I was not sure what I had let myself in for. I greeted them with another of my Italian words, I thought, but I think I said it in Spanish; they responded suitably and I gave them my name. I asked the Mother in French if this was a language that she understood. She replied, "Oui". Unfortunately that was the only word she knew in French. I now knew that this would be a challenge. With the help of reams of paper and lots of hand gestures, I found out what was needed. There was to be a family wedding in England and the Mother wanted the three little boys dressed in pin stripes, top hat and tails and the two little girls in Harrods' designed bridesmaids dresses. I began to rub my hands surreptitiously behind my back as I thought of all the commission that could be coming my way. I sent for the tailor to measure and design the suits for the boys and then sent for the dress designer and seamstress for the girls. I spent a whole working day with this family. Considering that we could not speak the same language I was highly delighted at the progress we all made. Not only was my confidence growing but so was my commission. I earned ten shillings by the end of the week. This was living in style. I had also gone up a peg or two in the eyes of the other staff and my Buyer.

Another of my regular customers was a Texas Rancher. He came to see me four times a year with a photograph of his four grand children. I then had to kit them out in English riding habit, doing my level best to guess the sizes required. He would appear at the end of the department in jeans, tasselled jacket, cowboy boots and Stetson. On spying me he would yell, "Well, hiyah honey, it's me again". The buyer wasn't too happy about him, but I was. Not only did I earn at least five pounds commission but he also took me out to lunch, having asked the buyer first. Being wealthy was something I could grow to like. What shall I do with a whole white five pound note? This was the amount of money that my Father sent to my Mother to keep the three of us for a month, which we managed to do, then.

My next excitement I hope will make all you lady readers sick with envy. I have lain on top of John Mills on the floor outside the packing room in Harrods. I had gone to the packing room to fetch some parcels for my previous customer. I came out on the run with my arms loaded with packages and I could not see where I was going.

I bumped into someone and the speed with which I was going knocked this person over backwards, and as I couldn't stop, I followed. I am now lying on top of this person, surrounded by parcels. Of course I apologised profusely and said, "Please lay still, and I will get the paramedics to check you over to see if there are any injuries". I looked at this man closely and I actually said, "Oh my god, you're John Mills". He replied, "Yes, and I have been for some time now". I told him that I was a fan of his, and I had seen many of his plays and films. I also informed him that his director was a personal friend of my Dad and I had performed to him in the living room. Unfortunately he had never offered me a part. I then spoke to John Mills and said, "Is there anything that I can do for you?"

He said, "Yes, get up". So without further ado, I did just that, dusted him off and we became good friends for the time I spent in Harrods.

Another occasion I heard via the grapevine that Tarzan was in the store; Gordon Scott not Johnny Weissmuller. I'm not that old.

I decided to dress up and took a child's coat from the rack, turned it inside out to reveal real leopard skin and tied it around my bosom. I took another coat and made a loin cloth. I then climbed onto a glass topped counter making suitable Tarzan noises whilst leaping from one counter to another. Who should appear in our department just at that moment was Tarzan. He reported me to not only the Buyer but to Sir Richard Burbidge for being insulting and demanded that I be sacked immediately. The Buyer appeased his temper and with only a small reprimand I was allowed to remain employed as long as I never served Tarzan dressed as Jane.

Living in Balham and travelling on the underground every day to and from work had its drawbacks. One day in a very crowded train I felt a cold hand on my thigh which then twanged my suspender. I had very little room to move so, what could I do? At the time I was carrying a box bag with four nice corners. As the train lurched I brought my bag to the front of my body and waited for the next opportunity. At the right moment I hit the gentleman in question in his credentials and watched as he fell to the floor in pain.

When the train reached the station he crawled onto the platform, gasping for breath and every one on the train applauded me. It was then that a few doubts crept into my mind. Supposing it hadn't been him. It could have been the man standing next to him.

Balham at the time was notorious for men of questionable morals.

One evening walking down the High street with a netball in a bag over my shoulder after a training session, I had this eerie feeling that I was being followed. So I did what most of us used to do, which was to stop and look in a shop window. Luckily he walked past me, disappeared and I said to myself, "Of course he's not following you".

As I turned down the next street to get home to Mum, this very man jumped out of a shop doorway with his trousers around his ankles and made a grab for me. My netball in the string bag came to the fore at this point. There was a very prominent target to aim for.

I ran like the wind to get home to safety. It's true what Confucius said, "That women can run faster with skirts up than men can with trousers down".

After two and a half years of Harrods I began to feel that if you didn't have money you were not worth speaking to. My family were not well off and I didn't like what I was thinking. So, I handed in my notice at the age of eighteen and a half.

What shall I do now? Whilst trying to make a decision I worked for a while at my local haberdashery shop. I was made to hand sew tickets on to all the clothes, doilies and cotton table mats. This was life in the raw and it didn't take me long to realise that this was not for me.

This is where my Fathers' influence came to the fore once again.

I asked him for help and advice. "Why don't you see if you can get a job with a bank?" he suggested. He was a brilliant mathematician but I was not and I felt that to be good at this subject was vital to be able to get employment in a Bank. He gave me the confidence to believe in myself so I sent in an application to join Lloyds Bank Limited at Southwark. To my surprise I passed the entrance exam and was given a starting date.

My first day at the Bank was what you would call, "In at the deep end". Everyone went down with the dreaded flu' and I was left alone with just the Manager, the Chief cashier, and one other staff member. I had to operate a National 32 Accounting Machine with only one day of training. There were times when I pressed all the wrong buttons and put all the accounts in the red.

To make matters worse I even sent out some of the statements to tell the customers of their financial situation. It wasn't until a few days had passed that I was summoned to the Managers office to meet one of the irate customers. He was the Managing Director of a very large firm, still in existence and I had informed their Company that they were 6 figures in the red, which was not true. It was at this time that I was able to use my sense of humour to its best advantage.

I, of course apologised profusely, whilst smiling and told him to shoot me down whenever he was ready. He accepted my apologies and did not take his account elsewhere.

Southwark Branch was quite small, only fourteen or fifteen staff.

Once everyone had recovered from the flu', I was sent to Lloyds Bank Training College, where much to my surprise, I became the top banking student of that year. I felt that at last I was going to be good at something.

I had a fabulous time at the branch as there was an awful lot of bum pinching that went on in the vaults. Today it would be known as sexual harassment, but, I enjoyed it. If I was bending down at a filing cabinet when one of the clerks walked by, I seemed to always get pinched. Not to be outdone, if he was bending down when I walked by, I would reciprocate. I can honestly say that this behaviour never went any further than described; it was just a silly bit of fun.

Our chief cashier was a gentleman called Mr. Penny. Very apt really as the country had not gone decimalised. Being the junior of the branch, it was my job Saturday lunchtime to lock up and make the Bank secure for the weekend. Everyone had left, so I proceeded to lock the outer door, to make sure no more customers could gain entry. I walked around checking the windows, doors and the vault. I then climbed the stairs out of the vault area and called in a very loud voice, "Has everyone gone?" I had no reply so I locked the bank for the weekend and went home.

When I came in Monday morning, Mr. Penny gave me the cold shoulder and wouldn't speak to me. I said, "What have I done to offend you? He said, "Where do you think I was when you locked the Bank for the weekend? I told him that I thought he must be halfway home to his wife and Saturday lunch. His reply stunned me. He said, "No; I was spending a penny and I did not hear you call. OOOOOeeeer!

I still, at the time lived at home with my Mother in Balham and we could not afford a telephone. The bank Manager was on a fishing weekend in Aberdeen. It took the police over three hours to find the other sets of key holders before they could release Mr. Penny. That cost me a bouquet of flowers for his wife to say sorry and a tin of Old Holborn for Mr. Penny's pipe. This lesson taught me that I could write odes. If you have a chief cashier called Mr. Penny and you lock him in the bank for the weekend whilst he is spending one, all the ingredients are there.

I requested one Saturday morning off as I needed to go to my Mothers' wedding. The Manager said that he always thought there was something different about me. I told him that this was her second time and I was not what he thought I was.

Some three years later I finally left the Bank as I was now married and wanted to be a part of my husbands' businesses.

We owned seven Hardware Retail outlets an Interflora Florist a Lawnmower Engineering workshop and our own Wholesale Company, whereby we purchased goods for over sixty other Independent Ironmongers.

After a few years study I became a professional lady Ironmonger and an Interflora Florist. I knew absolutely nothing about Lawnmowers. When they came in for repair and the customer would ask me what was wrong with it. I would always say, "It's probably carburettor problems". Even if it was a hand mower I would still say the same.

Suddenly finding that I was an Employer instead of an Employee was one of the hardest things to come to terms with. I wanted my staff to know that I was not the big bad boss and that I was the same as them. I just happened to be in the right place at the right time when I met my husband. I knew I had to let them know I had a sense of humour and would like them all to share it with me.

So, one day I put a two line ode on the counter to check on their reactions. It was very simple;
One of our suppliers left a lot of stock today,
Just see how much of these goods that you can put away.
It was three days before I received some replies thus;

Number 1.
We came in with the sun so gay,
And started putting things away,
We pushed and shoved, we heaved and puffed,
And now we think we've done enough.
And as you know the time flies by.
So now it's up to you……Goodbye.

Number 2.
Phew, it's been a hectic day,
Like a mad house, one might say,
Customers waiting at the door,
We've just had time to sweep the floor.
Rushing here, rushing there,
People spending without a care.
We've been as they say, as busy as bees,
And I've worn my legs down to my knees.

But although I'm glad the day is done,
I, must admit it's been quite fun.
So think of this day in years when I'm gone.
And remember me kindly as you quietly look on.
At the words on my tombstone neatly lacquered,
Here lies Eileen Bl…. knackered.
I had a strong feeling that my efforts had not been in vain.

One fine sunny spring day, I sold a rotary mower to my Dentist, whose practice was opposite my shop. As you can understand, I warned him of the dangers of such a machine. I told him to never walk backwards whilst mowing, as if you do and trip over falling backwards, whatever is in your hands will automatically come with you. Unfortunately he did not heed my warning. He was mowing his lawn, walking backwards and fell over a pile of bricks in his garden. You've probably guessed what happened next. Yes, you're right; the mower came with him and did severe damage to both feet.

He was rushed into Accident and Emergency where they tried to re attach the severed toes. We were all devastated at this piece of news and I wondered what on earth I could do to cheer him up. Not an easy task you might say.

The first thing I did was to put together a flower arrangement for him, as I owned a Florist shop this could be done quite easily. I went next door to the stationers and bought a get well card. I then took a tube of Evo-Stik off the shelf and placed that inside the card. I also attached an ode.

I send to you this tube of glue,
To make your toes as good as new,
And when next time you mow the grass,
Try not to fall upon your 'Arse'.

On receipt of this little memento, he told me later, that was the first time he had laughed in three days. The ode was circulated around the entire Hospital and was later published in the Medical Journal.

So as you can see it doesn't necessarily take a lot of money to cheer people up, just a bit of thought.

My family and I were now living in a four bedroom three reception room house with a large garden and double garage. Most of the rooms and the kitchen were in good decorative order but unfortunately the bathroom décor left something to be desired.

Being in the trade we ordered a new bathroom suite in Autumn Tan. This consisted of a toilet pan and seat, wash basin and taps and a very expensive cast iron bath. The plumbers started work, ripping out the old and putting in the new. Everything was going well until the delivery of the bath. This had those tiny pinholes in the casting, allowing the white colour underneath to show. As you can imagine, being a perfectionist we refused to accept second best. We must have sent this bath back to the factory on no less than three occasions, requesting one to be sent in a perfect condition to no avail. By now everything is fitted in the bathroom except the bath. It's at times like this that you find out who your best friends are. At least three times a week I would borrow a different friends shower or bath, just to try to feel clean. Our two sons were not in the least bothered if they couldn't have a bath.

I made numerous phone calls to the manufacturers and many polite letters were written but I don't think they were on my wavelength.

I knew that the answer would have to be an ode. This bath was made by Glynwedd Productions in South Wales, so I aimed the ode at them.

> Dear Mr. Glynwedd please help me you must,
> In you I have put all my faith and my trust.
> For three solid months now, I've not had a bath,
> If you think that's funny I dare you to laugh.
> The toilet is in and the wash basin too.
> I've tried, but I can't fit my feet in the loo.
> The tiles on the wall look so lonely and sad,
> If the bath was there too it wouldn't look bad.
> An effort is needed so please mend your ways,
> Remember the Universe took just seven days.

Forty eight hours later there was a knock on our front door. Outside was a large van with Bathroom Fittings written on the exterior.

We all came outside to inspect our bath, but before we could do that, four men climbed out of the van. They spread a carpet on the pavement and unloaded the bath. A blanket was put into the bath as the four men then proceeded to sit in the bath on the pavement outside our house and in unison they performed a foolscap ode from all the men on the factory floor. Not only were we entertained but the bath was billed to us at half price for making the factory floor ring to the sound of hilarity. I thought at this point, if I could find an ode for every situation perhaps I could get everything just that little bit cheaper. Laughter for me is proving to be a formidable ally.

I know that women are not as good as men when it comes to buying Ironmongery. We might know what the things do and how they do it but we never seem to know what the items are called. But of course we women are very good with our hands, so explaining what we needed using our two very good tools, became very important for both me and my customers.

We're not very good at measuring either are we? It's always too short, too long or ABOUT twelve inches. One of my regular customers asked me for a new clothes line and some expanding curtain wire. I said, "How long do you want the curtain wire?" She replied, "I need enough to cover the lavatory window". The second question, "How long do you need the clothes line?" She actually said, "I need it to stretch from the garage to the shed at the bottom of the garden". I had a lot of fun with this lady trying to determine how much of each item she needed.

Our Interflora Florist was a very busy outlet and we employed a full time lady driver.

One morning as we all came into work I noticed that she had been crying. I took her into the office, made her a cup of tea and asked her if she wanted to talk and tell me of the problem. We were both Mums, so I knew we could share children problems, if that was what it was about. She told me that one minute she was crying and the next minute she was giggling, even though the latter made her feel guilty. I asked her to share this problem. She said, "Well, you know I have a sixteen year old daughter who is at school with your two sons?" I replied that I did know this and that they were all good friends. "What is the matter?" Her answer bought me out in a cold sweat. She said, "My daughter is in the Maternity wing of the local hospital". "She is fine and so is the baby girl". I very quickly asked if the baby reminded her of either of my two sons. "Oh no", she said, "Neither of them are responsible". What a relief! I could now understand her tears and sadness. I said, "Well come on, what is there to laugh at?"

Her daughter, who was a Girl Guide, had gone away for the weekend with the Boy Scouts. In the early hours of one morning, the boys had joined the girls in the bell tent for a bit of extra curricular activity. None of them had bought any condoms, so they raided the kitchen tent and used cling film. I couldn't contain myself any longer and burst into hysterical laughter. It's difficult enough using it in the kitchen. The fact that both the daughter and the new baby were fit and well made the situation less critical.

The sequel to this episode is that a few days after hearing this story, our local Scout leader came to our shop with a long list of all he needed for a camp. At the very bottom of this list was two dozens rolls of Cling film. I obviously told him the story and suggested that he take foil instead.

Due to this episode my sales of Cling film dropped by 20%. I refused to sell it to anyone who couldn't prove they were over eighteen.

In the mid eighties I was voted the first and ever only lady to be President of the London and Southern Counties Ironmongers Association. What a title! This had a membership of some 5000, mostly men I hasten to add. I knew I would enjoy this task. I also had the dubious honour of being voted the first lady to serve on the Board of Management of the British Hardware Federation. I know that not many people have heard of these organisations, so you can deem from this snippet of information what a highly important person I was.

However in this capacity I had to attend and talk at all the meetings throughout London and Southern Counties, culminating at the end of my year of office to help organise a Conference to be held in Portugal.

One occasion saw me invited to Sheffield to address a group of Ironmongers on the subject of, "A woman in a man's world".

During the talk I pointed out that my husband and I had to get married on Wednesday afternoon as this was early closing day, therefore the takings wouldn't suffer. A young lady in the front row interrupted me and said, 'Aye lass I can beat thee, we got married Saturday morning before three as Sheffield United were playing at home". I didn't feel so hard done by after that comment.

Now being married we have two sons, one dog, three sets of puppies, two jobs and like all parents only one salary. When my sons were small and I couldn't go out very much, that's when I decided to teach myself to play the alto saxophone. My husband played the flute and the saxophone, so while he was at work I tried to learn. This proved fairly unsuccessful at first as I couldn't remember how to read music.

I started by buying a descant recorder and a book for young kids on how to play and read music. I progressed from a descant recorder to a treble and finally a base. I now felt that as the fingering for the saxophone was very similar to the recorders I should now be able to make music if the neighbours did not object. I succeeded in being able to master the technique of gaining the correct embouchure.

I have played my sax in a dance band, once; they never invited me back again. It was a great feeling to be on the stage helping the dancers to do a slow quickstep. The band leader's foot was tapping at speed and glaring at me, but I could not get the same speed as all the professionals. Could that be why I was never asked again? I have now also taught myself to play the guitar, the ukulele and the clarinet very badly. I'm very good on comb and paper and split peas in a Fairy liquid bottle.

Whilst my sons were learning Judo, I decided to learn Aikido. This is unarmed combat and it will teach me how to kill and maim in three easy lessons. Perhaps the local plumbers won't be so keen to take advantage of me with this knowledge under my belt.

Some men seem to think that women could not possibly know anything about plumbing.

One day our local plumber asked me if I sold connectors. I said that of course I did, do you want male or female? He grinned cheekily and said, "What's the difference?" I told my staff that I was going to take this man to the warehouse to explain the differences between male and female, and that should I not return within thirty minutes would you please come and rescue me. I have never seen a plumber run quite that fast before, but I think it taught him a lesson.

I have never used my knowledge of Aikido in anger. One summer evening, my eldest son, aged sixteen, had not arrived home by 11.00.p.m. and I was getting worried. My husband was ill in bed with the dreaded flu' so I got into our car and toured the streets looking for my stray. I found nothing, so now even more worried. I telephoned all the local hospitals and the Police station to see if they had heard of anything that might relate to my son. Again I drew a blank. By 1.30.a.m. I am distraught with worry and smoking heavily, parading up and down the area looking for my wayward son. Suddenly I see a person sauntering along the road as if it were five o'clock in the afternoon. It was my son. When he drew level with me I said, "Where the hell do you think you have been?" He said, "Mind your own b....y business". I immediately slapped him across his face, leaving my hand print, and told him to get indoors. He then turned on me and made two fists as if to hit me. I then put myself in the unarmed combat stance and said, "Go on then, I dare you". He ran indoors, up the stairs, locked himself in his room and never surfaced until late morning with an apology. I had been very nervous as to what he might do and how I would deal with it if he had attacked me. This was a first and a last.

My husband became a Rotarian and I an Inner Wheel Member.

I have done all the committee jobs at least three times and President of my club twice. I have spoken at the Blackpool Opera house in front of 5,000 Inner Wheel members at their Annual Conference. My subject was "Illegal Sunday Trading".

Every Christmas the Rotary Club would feed and entertain the senior citizens and us Inner Wheel girls would make the food and serve it. Entertainment followed after the meal had finished. On one such occasion, in my opinion, the show was so bad I opened my mouth saying, "If we can't do better than that, I'll eat my hat". Eating my words would have been a better option. I then formed my own troupe of players known as, The Hub and Spoke Players. Rotary, Inner Wheel Get it?

I wrote and produced shows not only for Rotary but for Inner Wheel the local hospitals and Senior Citizen homes for just over ten years until I ran out of steam and fresh ideas.

As a number of my customers were very deaf making communication nigh impossible, I decided to take some evening classes and learn British Sign Language for the Deaf. This is a seven year course which unfortunately I didn't complete. I managed two years only. But it has taught me how to communicate with people not as lucky as myself. After all we use sign language every day of our lives. I bet if someone stops you and asks for directions, if you had to keep your hands in your pockets it would be impossible. We waive at our friends which means Hallo. If you are female, young and good looking and sitting on a bar stool at the local pub and a young good looking male sits next to you, what do you do? You immediately cross your legs towards him and smile. This means, I fancy you, please buy me a drink and ask me for a date. If his girlfriend returns from the toilet, cross your legs away from him and try to find someone else.

In 1985 I made my parachute jump dressed as Wonder Woman, my son as Robin, a Rotarian as Batman and the newspapers sent me Superman disguised as Clark Kent. All the sponsorship money was paid into the bank under the name of a Charity and needed three signatures before any withdrawal could be made. The final total raised was two and a half thousand pounds.

One day my husband received a letter from the tax office as they thought that I had recently inherited this money, demanded half of it in Tax. I told him that there was no way they were going to get their hands on this money. It would be used for people much more needy than them. My Husband insisted that if the tax office demands it there is no way I can refuse. I said, "I have written them an ode".

He said, "You can't write the Tax Office an ode. I replied, "You're too late I have already 'wrut it and sent it".

> If all the money that I'd earn was underneath the bed,
> I wouldn't live in Ewell and at the Bank be in the red.
> But alas for me, you've noticed where I've hidden all the cash,
> I'm sorry no, not now, no time, I've really gotta dash,
> To foreign climes where income tax is not a dirty word,
> Or keeping all your hard earned cash is not thought so absurd.
> So come on all you Tax men, get your fingers off my dough,
> I've told you once; I've told you twice, the answer is still NO.

Did you know I never heard another word?

So should you get a Tax demand and don't want to pay it, let me know and I'll write you an ode.

By 1987 we decided to sell all the family businesses, due to falling customers, and trying to compete with the large D.I.Y Stores. We could always beat them on price but not on parking facilities.

Our Interflora Florist bought that Business and our Agricultural

Engineer bought the Mower Services Department, which is still going bearing our trade name.

My youngest son wanted to start his own business in Kitchen, Bedroom and Bathroom design. He taught me how to estimate, use a computer and how to measure accurately. I in turn taught him how to run a Business and make a profit. Sadly this was the time of a big depression and his business folded, but fortunately not losing out financially.

I was now unemployed and not sure what to do next.

Through our Rotary Club I was partially involved with helping to set up a Care at Home Service with the Leonard Cheshire Foundation.

You probably are aware that this provides care for disabled people enabling them to remain at home and still go to work if possible.

I very soon became totally hooked on this job and wanted to gain more qualifications. I gained my N.V.Q. care level grade three. I was qualified in moving and handling, health and safety, and received some training in physiotherapy. I finally became a Senior Care Attendant looking after clients with just physical disabilities. I was not qualified to deal with mental disabilities. I have been in this career for the past sixteen years.

Some of my friends seemed to think that this a very miserable job to be in. They couldn't be more wrong. I do feel that a sense of humour is obligatory and patience and understanding are a definite bonus. If you are of a condescending nature that job would not be for you.

One of my clients is a tetraplegic, that's paralysed from upper neck down. This was a result of an accident. One morning whilst getting him ready for the daily wash, I noticed that his private credentials were very red, sore and not a lot of skin to see. I winced in pain just to look. As he could feel nothing he asked me if I had hurt myself. I told him it wasn't my injury it was his. "What has happened," I asked. The incontinence sheaths that have to be worn contain self adhesive glue inside to make sure it stays where it should. A tube and leg bag is then attached to house the waste. An allergic reaction had taken place. I suggested that the local incontinence advisor be contacted to ask for some samples to find the right one suitable for him. He told me that he had written on a number of occasions to no avail. He asked me if I would write a suitable ode. How could I turn down such an auspicious request? I don't know what that means but it sounds intelligent.

Before I reached home the ode was composed.

> I hear that all your condoms come in sizes large to small,
> I wrote a letter weeks ago no response I've had at all.
> Your customer care is lacking and I don't know what to do,
> And if I was not disabled, then like you I'd use the loo,
> But as it is I'm wheelchair bound and need a helping hand,
> In choosing sizes best for me from small through large to grand.

Forty eight hours later, he received a large brown paper parcel containing every colour, shape and size, complete with measuring tool.

You'll be pleased to know we found a suitable one and the District Nurse solved the other problem.

Why is it that just because people can laugh it makes them respond?

Before I embark on any new adventure, I sit down and ask myself five very important questions.

1. Why am I going to do it?
2. How am I going to manage to do it?
3. Can I afford it?
4. Where on earth do I think I'm coming from?
5. Am I enjoying my journey in life so far?

* The answer to question one:
  'Cos it seemed like a good idea initially.

* The answer to question two;
  Now I am more mature, I will manage it, but slowly.

* The answer to question three;
  Of course I can. Pay for it now and worry about finances later.

* The answer to question four;
  Well, actually I come from Balham, on the Northern line.

* The answer to question five;
  Oh boy, Wow, yes, I am having a ball so far.

I have recently discovered that by the time I have asked all these questions and then found the answers, it's too late. On reaching number five I have usually embarked on the next adventure.

I am the same now as I have always been, except older but not necessarily wiser.

My Mum told me that I would be a trial and tribulation to everyone that knew me. I think she has been proved right so far.

My family told me that if ever you do anything as dangerous again as learning to fly at the grand age of fifty six, we'll kill you.

I don't think they meant it seriously though.

THE PETTICOAT PILOT

It began one cold miserable day in one of my Hardware stores. The sort of day when you're cold, hungry, and you can't wait for 5.30.p.m. to come and something exciting to happen.

A young Rep. called trying to sell me his wares and during the conversation, mentioned that recently he had made a parachute jump for Charity. He needed to say no more.

Some six months later, dressed as Wonder Woman, my son as Robin, a rotarian as Batman and the newspapers sent me Clark Kent (heavily disguised as Superman), I made a Parachute Jump from Headcorn in a twin engine Islander.

This aircraft was blue and it had two things that go round at the front, (my total knowledge of airplanes).

Getting prepared for the leap into space was nerve racking and exciting.

Once our party was fitted with parachutes and ready to go we were told to sit outside on the bench and wait for our number to be called.

On this bench I was the only woman amongst 6 men, so when we were called I quickly ran to the front of the line. Women and children first. This

Wonderwoman, Batman, Robin - the parachute jump

Twin Engined Islander, Headcorn - for parachute jump

was a bad mistake, as I was immediately asked to go the rear of the line. Very indignantly I asked "Why". I was told it was because I was the only woman. As this was the case, I was to be last on, first out.

"Why is that so important?" I asked . The jumpmaster came back with a very quick response. "As you are the only woman, providing you jump all the men will automatically follow, not wishing to be outdone by a mere woman".

As I walked to the aircraft I noticed there were many pieces of black sticky tape holding the airframe together. There was no door, only a large hole where it should have been. I asked the jumpmaster to explain. I was informed that there was no point in leaving the door on, as he would only have to open it before I could jump. He had removed it and left it in the hangar. Oh boy was I feeling brave at this point.

The aircraft had no seats, so we sat on the shiny lino and clipped our parachutes on the overhead cables. When we were all pronounced ready, the aircraft took off. As we reached the height of 2,000 feet the plane banked very sharply to the left to come in over the drop zone. This is where my shiny jump suit acted very badly on the shiny lino and I slid towards the place where there should have been a door.

The only thing that kept me aboard was the jumpmaster's leg across the doorway, which as you can imagine, now had severe fingernail indentations in his shins.

He screamed at me to shuffle my bottom a bit further forward. I am now sitting in the doorway with my legs dangling down over 2,000 feet of nothing.

I could see all my family and all my friends looking skyward. Some fifty Rotarians had come along to support this venture. Even to the point of bringing a blackboard and easel, where they were taking bets on how long it would take me to reach the ground.

This ranged from 3 minutes to 35 seconds DEAD. Which of course I was not.

The traffic lights beside me came on RED, AMBER then GREEN. The jumpmaster slapped me on the shoulder and screamed JUMP.

This is where I declined his offer. But guess what, I was not in the plane any more. I think he pushed. So I performed what I had been taught.

I put myself into the star position and screamed "One thousand, Two thousand up to five thousand, then checked to see if I had a canopy. This is quite important at this stage. If the answer is in the negative I have three seconds to make up my mind before deploying my reserve chute. Should I have waited four seconds, I might have been examining every blade of grass very closely. Fortunately I had a good canopy and then began to float very gently to the ground. That was great. So quiet, peaceful and beautiful.

Before long I noticed something else. The ground seemed to be coming up fairly quickly. I thought, get ready, this might hurt.

When I was 20 feet from the ground there was another jumpmaster with a megaphone looking up at me and shouting instructions. To make sure I would land safely, he said, "For heavens sake put your knees together." I actually thought they were. "Put your chin on your chest". "Is there anything you can do about the size of your chest?" I promised to sort him out when I landed.

I was now coming down in the field exactly where I should be, but what I hadn't noticed was that the field was full of sheep. I shouted at the jumpmaster, "What shall I do about the sheep?" He suggested that I open my legs. I said, "You have just said, put your knees together." He said, "Don't argue, you are only 10 feet from the ground". "O.K., what shall I do now." I was told to look down and yell out "Mint Sauce". In my fright I did just that. Fortunately they all ran away and I missed every one of them. I think it would have been a softer landing if I had landed astride a woolly jumper.

We had had a very long hot dry summer. When you leap from an aircraft at 2,000 feet, by the time you hit the deck, under normal weather conditions, you are travelling at about 15 miles an hour, which doesn't sound too fast. I landed on all the dried sheep's turds. It was just like landing on Brighton beach.

Fortunately my son and I landed safely, but unfortunately both Batman and Superman did severe ankle damage and were whisked off to hospital to be treated.

WOW! Wonder Woman came out on top.

Over £2,500 was raised for local Charities, including the Leonard Cheshire Foundation. We helped people do the things that some of us can take for granted. For example, go to the supermarket, have a haircut, go to the pictures, theatre or go away for a weekend.

I was well and truly hooked, not on parachuting, which was far too dangerous, but I felt an overwhelming desire to learn to fly a light aircraft.

My desires had to be curbed until 1987 when the businesses were finally sold and more time was available for me to pursue one of my dreams. At last I was out of debt, out of work and out of danger. Well for the time being.

As I recovered, I started to look for excitement once again. I applied for several jobs, was accepted for some and turned down by as many others for being a "Smart Arse". I finally settled for working for my youngest son and his partner, in their Kitchen, Bathroom and Bedroom Studio, with a new career to learn. I taught my son how to run a business whilst he taught me how to measure, estimate and use a computer. But still I needed some excitement.

One day while typing estimates and sipping a hot cup of tea and day dreaming I recalled my short flight in a light aircraft and how exciting it had been. I grabbed the "Yellow Pages" turned to "F" for Flying Schools," "B" for Biggin Hill, took my courage in both hands and picked up the phone. This would be exciting! I felt just like a kid waiting for Santa Claus to come down the chimney.

The day of my first flight came at last! I arrived at Biggin Hill for my "Land away Double". I was instructed on the ground with the aid of a model aircraft to illustrate what happens when you move this, or waggle that, something to do with ailerons causing rolling, elevators causing pitching and the rudder causing yawing. I nodded intelligently when asked if I understood.

With my first ground briefing finished 'flight plan' completed, I made a final visit to the loo. The weather was checked, my headset was at the ready and my hair was combed. My fingernails were varnished and my high heels in place. As my make up was in good condition, we walked onto the airfield, where I immediately lost my high heels in the mud and ruined my nail polish. I then climbed high on the wing of the aircraft and bent down to open the canopy.

Airfields are notoriously windy aren't they? The wind took my full skirt and petticoat over my head revealing all my worldly goods to the boys of Biggin Hill School of Flying. I heard them say, 'Take a look at this fellas". I panicked a little because I could not remember whether I had put any underwear on that day. So what, they knew what I was made of now. It was at this time that I learnt my first lessons in aviation. Never wear nail polish, high heels or a flared skirt when flying.

I sat in the cockpit, which I discovered, is flying terminology for the driving seat. I tried to look nonchalant as the Pilot walked around the plane, moving this, wiggling that and testing the other. I was *impressed*! He then climbed aboard, helped me "Belt up", showed me where to plug in my head set and we were nearly ready to go, I thought…*but then you know what thought did.*

After what seemed like an eternity, the engine began to throb noisily and all my bits began to wobble uncontrollably. The Pilot broke into a foreign language, talking to someone at Biggin Control Tower. They must have been of the same nationality as they immediately answered him in the same foreign tongue. It was then that we started to move. This is it, you lucky devil. We're off.

How wrong can you be?

We drove to a holding point where *power checks* were completed, whatever they are, and after another ten minutes began to move yet again. This, I now know is called Taxiing. I hope you are suitably impressed as to how quickly I can pick up the correct jargon.

We have now lined up on the runway and have been given permission to TAKE OFF.

With one last check of *all* the instruments, the brakes were released and we sped along the runway, taking off very smoothly into the unknown. The instructor asked me if I would like to take control. I replied in the affirmative as I had paid him a lot of money for the privilege. I put my left hand on the controls. He said, "It's not obligatory for your knuckles to be that white". I relaxed my grip.

So, somewhere over England I was allowed to bank left and right, to climb and to dive. I was already an ace pilot. This was going to be easy, I thought. About 1 hour later we landed at Elstree where we had a well-earned cup of coffee and a very urgent trip to the usual offices, before taking off again to return to Biggin Hill.

I was given a lot more *hands on* experience and finally I landed the plane with verbal instructions and *some* help from a fairly jumpy instructor. I am told that he is getting better quite quickly and will be released fairly soon.

On touch down my instructor said, "Do you know the measure of a good pilot?"

"How can I?" I said, "This is my first time with hands on and my first time ever in a light aircraft.

He told me that the measure of a good pilot is one who has the same number of take-offs as landings. All landings are controlled crashes and providing you can walk away from one it's been a good'un.

By now I was convinced that anyone could learn to fly. With the minimum number of lessons, I would soon be a fighter pilot or just cruising on my own over the English Countryside. Pride always goes before a fall, or should I say fool. Little did I know what lay ahead of me, but I was soon to find out.

I continued to fly once a month, sometimes as little as every six weeks for the next twelve months, when my instructor resigned. To this day I am not sure whether it was something I said or something I did. A whole year had been wasted. Not flying regularly was unacceptable: as each lesson was forgotten by the time I flew again, so…with a brand new instructor, very much poorer in pocket, I started again with an enthusiasm and determination that would have made Douglas Bader proud of me.

Just because at the time I was a fifty-two-year old woman on H.R.T. and knew nothing about four stroke piston engines, nothing about Aerodynamics, Navigation, Meteorology (let alone say it), Aircraft Technology, Mathematics, or the process of learning, I had decided that this was not going to stand in my way.

I sold the shares my Dad had left me when he died in 1974 and began to learn to fly, whereas before, I was just having flying lessons. The first set of hurdles I had to overcome was:-

- To not only be able to control the damn thing on the ground but in the air as well.
- To make a safe landing….every time and more importantly, to be able to walk away afterwards.

Before I could fly my first solo, I needed to pass a full Medical and my Air Law examination. Luckily, I passed my medical.

Once you are over 50, a medical has to be passed every year, with such things as an E.C.G. Blood Test, Eye test and Urine test.

The Air Law Exam is very important. This teaches you whose airspace you are in. If you are a light aircraft and you stray into Heathrow zone, they get very cross.

If I am going to make a mistake, I usually *do it big*. I had the Mayor of our town on board who used to be a friend of mine. I was going to fly over Guildford Cathedral. We were chatting to each other as you do, when you have nothing else to do but fly. The weather was beautiful, blue sky, sunshine but only one cloud. It chased me. I flew into it. I was now flying on instruments to get out of the cloud and on doing so, the Mayor looked down and said, "Ooh, look that's Brooklands". This is five miles inside the Heathrow traffic zone. The Mayor told me he had his A-Z on board and asked if it would be of any help to me.

I have since spoken to the Ministry of Transport and they have offered to make the road signs bigger and the boys have painted on the hangar roofs, Ann we're over here".

Taking my Air law Exam was a terrifying ordeal, my first exam since leaving school I had to work very hard trying to remember, which can fly where, at what height and in what air space. I also needed to learn what certificates that the pilot and the aircraft need, and what NOTAMS are.

Such a lot to learn, If I fly V.F.R. which stands for Visual Flight Rules, I have to look out of the window and make sure I do not hit another aircraft coming in the opposite direction. Hitting another aircraft is not good! It would mean immediate failure not to mention the examiner very cross, should he survive!

I must not fly at night or in clouds. All pilots fly from the left seat, so if I want to I can navigate by straight-line features, keeping them on my left, like railway lines (if there are any left), rivers, canals and coastlines. The M25 is a very good feature, nothing moves, so I know it's the M25.

One day I was doing just that, flying alongside the M25, with it on my left, when Thames Radar called and said, "We have another aircraft, at your height coming towards you, do you have him on visual?" Why don't they say, CAN YOU SEE IT?

I replied, "That is a negative, but you will be the first to know when I have it on visual". Some ten minutes later the aircraft passed me on the other side of the M25, going in the opposite direction. Luckily for me he had passed the same exam. If he had not, then I could never tell anyone this story.

You know the Motorway is never as wide as you think it is…well, my first instinct at this time was to breathe in. Not a lot of good really.

Eventually, I took the exam and passed with flying colours…Sorry for the pun.

I was now ready for my first Solo, but one obstacle remained in my way. I could not consistently land safely and failed to see what I was doing wrong. Until I could master this difficult technique I was going nowhere, well not on my own. So far I had performed more go-a-rounds, balloons and bounces than any other four students. I knew it would come right soon.

Some 12 months later one hot sunny August afternoon I was yet again, performing circuits and bumps. After just ten minutes of flying, my instructor said, "O.K. you can take me down now". I protested that my lesson had not finished and demanded my monies' worth. "*I am going to send you on your first solo,*" he said. How I managed to land safely, I do not know, but land I did.

I taxied to the school and received a few last words of encouragement. My instructor left the plane and there I was, all alone on the taxiway ready for an adventure. There was no time to even spend a penny. My hands began to shake and my mouth became very dry. My lips stuck to my teeth and my legs did not appear to be attached to my body. This had to be the loneliest place on the face of the earth. The Tower was informed that this was my first solo and had agreed to look after me. I took a deep breath and began all the checks. Then to be sure, I did them all again and when I felt that all was O.K. I called for taxi instructions.

My call sign was GOLF BRAVA CHARLIE TANGO ALPHA. Quite simple really, but what I actually said was: - "This is Golf Bravo Charlie Angle Talpha, can I have Tango instructions?" Realizing what I had said I transmitted the words OOOPS. I cannot find that in the manual anywhere. I very quickly informed the tower and all other pilots listening, that I knew how to Tango but could you give me taxi instructions instead. I was already feeling better as I had broken the tension with a laugh.

I was given clearance to take off and as I sped up the runway I can remember shouting out loud "OH S! There's another fine mess you've got yourself into". The next 15 minutes was not only the longest, but also the most exhilarating and exciting 15 minutes I have ever spent in my entire life. I doubt if that feeling will ever return. Joy mixed with terror and the sheer exuberance of flying an airplane on your own for the first time cannot be described. It has to be experienced.

All too quickly the circuit was completed and I knew the critical test had arrived. My next task was to land safely and walk away, so that I could brag to all my family and friends. I was cleared to land, but experienced great difficulty in controlling the aircraft. My palms were sweaty; my hair was soaked with perspiration causing the headset to fall over my eyes. The temperature in the cockpit was 87°. "You can do it girl," I could hear my Dad saying. "Remember, genius is 10% inspiration and 90% perspiration." At last I understood that well-known saying. It was then that my life flashed before me. Was I going to live or die? Did I tell my two sons which knicker draw my Will was in? Have I turned off the gas and is the back door locked? Stupid woman I thought, concentrate on the job in hand.

To land safely there are a number of vital checks that must be done when you are *downwind*. Being very nervous I knew that I would never remember everything. Fortunately I had managed to find a mnemonic to help me with this task.

- **"B". Brakes.**
- **"U" Undercarriage.**
- **"M". Mixture.**
- **"F". Fuel.**
- **"A". Altitude.**
- **"R". Radio.**
- **"T". Temperatures.**

"B.U.M.F.A.R.T". How could I forget what to do downwind with that word going through my thoughts?

There are a few other things that need to be done but if you remember the mnemonic there is a good chance that you will land and be able to walk away. Then quite suddenly I was on the ground, alive and in one piece. The Tower called and congratulated me, I screamed with excitement, telling myself that I was alive and brilliant. Then I forgot to put the brakes on and immediately overshot my turning point on the runway and got lost…

Such humiliation.

I called the Tower and asked them where to go. Being the nice people that they are, they told me. "There is a blue and white striped Piper Cherokee in front of you… do you have him on visual?"
Why can't they just say, "Can you see it?"

I confirmed I had it on **visual** as "Can you see it" is not in the manual. Still very confused, I followed the Cherokee, which fortunately was going in the same direction.

Back at the flying school I parked the plane between two others. Wing tip to wing tip. I thought parking my car was hard. All the boys at Biggin Hill were there to meet me. When I signalled that the aircraft was shut down and completely safe, they ran up both wings to congratulate me.

I had to be helped from the aircraft as my legs had now gone on strike permanently. Champagne was served, photos were taken to record this momentous occasion, a certificate was issued and my debriefing session took place in a fog of euphoria and alcoholic stupor. The boys at Biggin Hill were marvellous to me: they never made me feel like a woman in mid-life crisis, or that I should be at home knitting or crocheting. I was then presented with a gift-wrapped parcel from the boys. WOW. How thoughtful. I THOUGHT. Then I opened it. Inside was a clean pair of knickers and a toilet roll. I could now see the calibre of the boys I would be working with at Biggin Hill.

My logbook now records 15 minutes as Captain-in-Command.

FIRST FLIGHT

Certificate

This is to Certify that

Ann Chance

has completed their **FIRST FLIGHT** in a
**Cessna Aircraft and has controlled
the aircraft from the pilot's seat.**

At Biggin Hill

On 16th May 1989

Signed _____ Instructor

LSF   **DSF**   **BHSF**   **BSF**

London School of Flying   Biggin Hill School of Flying
Denham School of Flying   Blackbushe School of Flying

After this there would be no stopping me or so I thought…My instructor soon brought me down to earth with a big bump. "O.K" he said, "Have you started studying for your Meteorology exam?" Clever clogs I thought, he knows I haven't. Did you know there are five different types of

41

fog? Cyclones, Anti-cyclones, Thermals, Updrafts and winds of all types. There are many types of clouds some in America called Mammary's. Their very name explains their shape. There are weather systems called, CAVOK, TEMPOS, PROBS, and RAPIDS. All of this is summed up in one word. WEATHER (To fly or not to fly).

Eventually, after many hours of night school, I took my courage in both hands and sat the Meteorology exam. I passed first time. I was really winning now.

I learnt some fascinating things about the weather. Do you know the difference between fog and mist? It's one kilometre. This knowledge can be used at a dinner party if the conversation goes a bit stale around pudding time, tell your guests this vital piece of Meteorological knowledge and suddenly everyone will offer to wash up.

After flying more than five and a half hours *completely alone,* around the circuit of Biggin Hill aerodrome, I was getting fed up with the monotony. With all my circuits completed, I was slowly beginning to believe that my goal was getting nearer. I had flown sideways, slowly, quickly and stalled at a great height. Practiced forced landing in a field with engine failure and even flown to Le Touquet for lunch and back again with four other students and their instructors.

On this occasion I was allowed to be Squadron Leader. As we were a foursome I suggested we fly in a diamond formation at least a mile apart. I could begin to like this life style.

The next task was to study for my Navigation Exam.

A Particular occasion I will not forget was my second flight alone called a Land Away Single where I had to turn my back on Biggin Hill, navigate and find an airfield, land, get marked on airmanship, approach and return to base.

That feeling of desperation was hard to come to terms with.

I chose Lydd as I felt that anyone could find this. It is on the edge of England, with a coastline and an enormous Atomic Power Station, which *should be* impossible to miss. I worked out my navigation route and with confidence took off. In a short while I was at the coast. I could see the sea, the power station, but not the runway! I called the control tower and informed them as to who I was and my position and that I did not have the runway on visual would they please assist.

Their actual words to me were as follows;

"It was there this morning"

I decided to orientate. It sounded good but I wasn't sure what it meant.

I had read it in one of my books. On tipping my right wing down I could see the runway was beneath me. I happily called the tower and told them that I now had their runway on visual, would they give me joining and landing instructions. Their reply again was memorable; "You may come in any way you like you are the only idiot up there today!"

A number of my friends ask me how you know when you are over the coast of France. Of course it is very simple, you fly to Lydd, because I know where that is now, and you leap off the edge of England. If there is sea underneath you, you are probably going roughly in the right direction. After some 30-40 minutes the next time you speak to an air traffic

Me at Biggin Hill

controller, if they say something like, "HAW HI HAW HI HAW", you are most certainly over the coast of France. If the reply is "ACHT TUNG", you are slightly wrong, so turn left a bit and you will soon find France.

The next hurdle I had to overcome was to *pass* the Navigation exam. Navigation has always been a mystery! I was now attending evening and Sunday classes. I had to learn about closing angles, how to find the direction of the Wind and how to use a Circular Slide Rule and Protractor.

My Father had been a Mathematician and many times tried to teach me how to use and understand a slide rule, which I never mastered. Learning to not only use, but also to interpret what I had worked out on the circular slide rule was very difficult. I finally mastered this difficult piece of equipment to discover that, it would also tell you where your wind is coming from. As we are all troubled by the wind and need to know where it is coming from, this is an important tool.

To be able to interpret what I saw on the ground and match it to what

I could see on the chart. I had to learn about Headings, Tracks, and Magnetic Tracks. Maximum safe altitudes, planned altitudes, E.T.A'S, V.R.P'S, V.O.R'S and V.I.P'S whilst also *flying* the plane! This was a new language for me to learn, everyone spoke in initials.

One day during navigation exercise, totally confident and feeling very proud of myself, my instructor asked me if I knew where I was. In the plane? I informed him that this was an affirmative as all pilots are never lost. I was temporarily uncertain of my geographical location. He asked me to tell him the name of the river below. I announced that it was the River Thames and his remark was, "Very good". The next question was, "What is that bridge over there?" Very confidently I said, "The new Queen Elizabeth Bridge at Dartford".

Again he said, "Very good. Now if that is where you are please navigate your return to Biggin Hill". One hour later I landed in Leicester. This is known as a learning curve. These silly mistakes and MANY, MANY, more beside are all par for the course in learning how to navigate your way around the globe.

The pace was now hotting up. Every lesson we flew away from base on a Navigation exercise. I was now not only expected to fly the plane, navigate, enjoy the view, answer technical questions, find home and land safely as well.

Just to keep me on my toes, I was also learning, what to do with an engine fire on the ground, or in the air, plus engine failure on take off or in flight. This I found exciting, but there are many local farmers who will never again plough their fields without looking cautiously skyward or wearing a hard hat. Even a few workmen on the M25 have had to run for cover.

After hours of study and many sleepless nights, one Sunday morning I decided that today would be the day I would sit the Navigation exam. I collected my tools, pens and rulers, and walked into the exam room on my own. I was so nervous I could not hold my pen still. Every Navigation line I tried to draw became a wiggle. The calming voice of my sister, who is a math's teacher, came to me, "Pen down Ann, take a deep breath, read all the questions, think of England and then begin again." Begin again I did and finished with another good pass. My instructor had said before the exam, "Ann always remember R.T.F.Q...Read the Flipping Questions". Or words to that effect.

If I thought Navigation was hard, Aircraft Technology was totally beyond me. I had to learn what made the plane fly, what keeps it up there and just as important what brings it down. If only I had listened to my Lawn-Mower Engineer I would have known that a four stroke piston engine cycle is Suck, Squeeze, Bang and Blow. But then who cares? Perhaps if you are at a dinner party and you have already told your guests about the difference between fog and mist; try teaching them the cycle of a four stroke piston engine. What fun.

I knew that a carburettor was important but not why? Did you know that a gyro could topple during aerobatics?

Until now I had always thought that an engine was just the noisy bit in front of an airplane, while it performed there was no need to be concerned.

How naive could I be?

I soon found out when the day came to take the exam, but I passed with 89%. Not bad for an idiot was it?

I was now getting ready for my first solo cross-country flight. In other words, that means flying away from home with two turning points and then finding my way back. A total of about one hour's solo flight. The day it all happened was just like any other to begin with, my instructor Simon took me for a short flight and then declared I was ready. Some folks enjoy watching you suffer, don't they?

My route was to leave Biggin Hill, turn my back on safety and home, fly to Ticehurst via Seven Oaks and Gravesend, and then return to Biggin Hill, if I could find it. With only one small hiccup, which I am prepared to admit, I made it back home and landed safely. After congratulations, I was treated to a celebratory drink at the Cabair Club House. What a moment! By which time I had uncrossed my legs and my knuckles were no longer white.

The next hurdle was to perform a Land Away Double alone.

This meant I had to leave Biggin Hill, land at two other airfields, namely Lydd and Southampton, getting marked on the way and finally land safely back at base.

The original route planned had to be scrapped as the weather was too awful to fly where I had intended. Hurriedly I worked out a new flight plan, got it checked with my instructor and began performing all the necessary bits and pieces.

I was now airborne, and on my way to land safely, I hoped, at Southampton, but experienced some trouble in finding it. I was going in the wrong direction. So swallowing my pride I had to ask for help, which fortunately was freely given. I knew this would blow my chances of passing that bit of the test. My heart rate increased and so did my blood pressure. Undaunted after landing eventually at Southampton and having a very strong cup of coffee and a very urgent trip to the loo.I checked my navigation and took off for Lydd. I enjoyed this leg as I had decided to fly along the coast. A truly magnificent view. I found the runway without any difficulty, as I knew where it was from past experience. On landing at Biggin Hill I was told by my instructor that I had passed some of the test but not all. A few days later I flew the test again and managed to find and land at Southampton without any help at all.

During my learning phases there have been frequent scares, one of which is still very fresh in my mind. Sitting on the runway I was given clearance to take off. I had just passed the point of no return when my air speed indicator failed and shot back to zero. My instructor took over the controls and climbed the aircraft to 1000 feet, handed me back the controls and said, "What are you going to do now Ann?" In my opinion all flying instructors have "A" levels in sadism.

I informed the tower, after I had had a mild panic attack and told them of my predicament. They cleared the runway and told me to land as soon as possible. Now… you do not need to know much about flying to know that air speed indication is vital. All I could do to make a safe landing was to operate from what I could hear, see or feel. I now know what it is like to fly by the seat of my pants. About 50 feet from the ground I said to my instructor, "you had better take over here; I have never landed an aircraft before not knowing the air speed". He replied, "That's funny, neither have I. If you do it, I'll watch and if it gets life threatening, I promise I will help you". Fortunately, I landed safely without any help from my instructor. I taxied back to the flying school where all the other pilots had assembled to offer help to find the cause of the problem.

On investigation, we found a very dead wasp in the Pitot tube. This is a small tube under the wing with a hole at one end, up which the air is driven in flight. The gauge then measures the difference between static and dynamic pressure and thus records the air speed. No hole, no air speed. Weight Watchers please note, this is a good method of losing weight.

To my knowledge I am the only student at Biggin Hill whose logbook records, "Flight aborted due to wasp up Pitot tube". Some people in life get all the good fortune.

The last but one written exam has now been passed. This was called "Human Factors for Pilots". A study of people under stress and how to deal with the associated problems that may arise. Whoever suggested that becoming a Pilot would be easy?

A few years ago I had the good fortune to be invited to speak to aircrew from World War II at Fairoaks airport. The Air-Vice Marshall had flown in just to listen to me. Amongst some of the items I produced was the book called "Human Factors for Pilots". Practically every pilot in the room shouted at me and said, "It's not true". I said confused, "What's not true?" "No pilots are human," they shouted.

Now there was only one last written exam to go, Radiotelephony. Without this exam under my belt, no further progress would be possible. There are two parts for this test, a written and an oral exam. I must have the correct set of teeth for this one.

By now I had passed all my written Exams and I held a Radio License, but could still not call myself a Pilot....YET.

To fight my way towards my goal, I worked very hard as a Senior Care Attendant for the Leonard Cheshire Foundation called Carewell, Family support, based in Epsom. This was founded with the help of the Ewell Rotary Club and the Doctors and Nurses at our Clinic. My day started at 7.30.a.m. looking after a young Solicitor whose neck was broken in a Rugby accident some ten years ago. Support is also given to a family in the evening, whose seven year old son was born with Cerebral Palsy.

I have many other clients from severe Tetraplegics and Paraplegics, to M.S. sufferers of all ages and sexes. Carewell also look after many clients with crippling Arthritis.

My full time employment in my sons showroom started at 9.00.a.m. and finished at 5.30.p.m. Among other activities I was Treasurer of our Inner Wheel Club and Secretary to the Ewell Chamber of Commerce. Rich and lazy I was not. Hard working and stupid, well, that's a different matter. At the end of the day I enjoy a very busy life, which is of my choosing.

To get just this far with my flying, there have been many hours of hard work, dedication, disappointment, frustration, tears, tantrums and the careless spending of money. Wonderfully dedicated young men about the ages of my two sons have taught me to fly. We have built up a good relationship, friendship and understanding. Flying has taught me a lot about myself, my short comings, self discipline and what makes me tick. I have also discovered that flying is addictive and I can now truly say that at the grand age of fifty-five... I am an addict. I can't wait for the day when I can proudly say I have a P.P.L. Private Pilots License. My dream comes true.

On the 10th March 1993, I was due to take yet another flying lesson.

Since Christmas Eve I had been waiting for a suitable day, weather wise, on which to take my LAST TEST; The General Flying Test. One of those terrifying occasions, when everything you have learnt about your particular subject has to be strung together in one great show of competence. I took my instructor flying, where I performed all that was requested and even some things that were not. All was going well.

My instructor was impressed.

"Let's land now," he said, "I've seen enough. You are ready to take your finals".

He informed me that he had taken the liberty of sending for a Civil Aviation Authority Examiner who was now waiting for me at the school.

Surprise tactics I've always thought to be a good thing and I was given no time to get "Wound up". I was introduced to Gordon, a nice man, in fact a very, very, nice man. Did he realize he would be risking his life and limb by putting me through my paces?

My first job was to make a visit to the usual offices in preparation for what might happen next.

I had to weigh the aircraft, the oil and the fuel, him and me. Next I had to work out the centre of gravity envelope to make sure we were light enough to take off and more importantly, light enough to land safely.

I then obtained a full meteorological report of any area that he might take me to. What to do if the runway is wet or covered in snow. What are my take off distances and what are my landing distances?

I was very pleased that all these tests were to the examiners satisfaction.

He then told me which aircraft we would be flying and requested that I "Do the outside visual checks".

I was only half way round the aircraft when he joined me. I told him I was sorry but that I hadn't finished yet.

He said, "No problem, please demonstrate your knowledge of this particular aircraft". What on earth did he want to know?

Being very nervous it was at this point that my sense of humour took hold of me.

I said, "This is a 4 seater single engine Grumman Cheetah".

He replied, "Very good, but it does say that on the side of the plane".

I told him the plane had two wings and demonstrated by holding my arms out sideway. I informed him of the position of the ailerons and what they did, the flaps, the elevator and the rudder. I felt very proud of myself, as he looked quite impressed. I asked him to "Walk this way to the front of the plane please".

"This", I said, "is the nose wheel, because it's under the nose and held together by Olio Struts". He asked me, "What are they?" "I'm not sure, I read all about it in a book", I said. I pointed out the propeller and when the engine is switched on will rotate in a clockwise direction. If it goes the other way, it might mow the grass at the same time. I then opened the cowling and showed him the engine. I actually told him that its cycle is Suck, Squeeze, Bang and Blow.

He said, "No other student has ever told me that".

I said, "Some of us have it, some of us don't".

After briefing, paper work, aircraft documents checked, aircraft safety checked, I was now in readiness for one of the most important moments of my life.

At 2,400 feet, which is 100 feet below Gatwick/Heathrow zone, I performed everything he asked me to do. I flew high and low, slow and fast, many different landings, some with flaps and some without. I had to perform a landing on the runway without power.

I was halfway downwind doing my checks when he took the power off and said, "Oh dear, you have an engine failure, please land on the numbers on the runway". On his command, I performed stalls with flaps and without, an engine failure on take-off and 45 degree turns left and right.

I executed an engine failure at height and had to find a field in which I could land if necessary. At 500 feet I managed to convince the examiner that this was possible and he let me climb away. I think the farmer below me thought he was going to get a furrow where he hadn't planned one.

I then had to perform many functions by flying only on instruments. The examiner had forgotten the eye shields, which is a pair of glasses with the top half blackened and clear glass at the bottom. This would enable me to read the instruments but not see the horizon. I fly the plane and he acts as my eyes. He put his anorak over the windscreen and made me promise not to cheat.

I then had to demonstrate orientation. If only I could remember what it meant.

Throughout this time it was important to keep smiling and sound confident.

One task was to climb to 4000 feet, take the power off and go into a flat spiral dive. For this manoeuvre he gave me 250 feet to correct the situation. As I came out of the spiral he told me that I had gone a strange colour and asked if I was alright. He asked me to look out of the cockpit fairly soon. I said "Is there a problem". He said, "Yes, the horizon is nearly vertical" I knew I felt giddy, but I didn't think I was that bad.

Eventually I straightened the aircraft until I had a horizontal horizon. The gyros had toppled and nothing seemed to be right. So I flew straight and level for 10 minutes putting everything in its rightful place until I was satisfied.

After an hour and a half in the air I was told that if I could find Biggin Hill runway and land safely, *"You have passed."* For four years I had worked very hard to hear those three little words. Then the doubts began to creep in. Suppose I cannot find Biggin Hill. Suppose I crash on landing. Come on Ann, I told myself, you have done this hundreds of times. You are not going to fluff it now.

The examiner asked me if I knew where I was.

Obviously I replied with the old adage that, "All pilots are never lost, I am temporarily uncertain of my geographical location". He suggested that I orientate. If only I could remember what that word meant.

After orientating I spied Sevenoaks.

I reported this and told the examiner, "I have Sevenoaks 30 degrees on my port side. I know that is on my left because Granddad said, there is no port left 'cos your Grandmother has drunk it all." He said, "I'll make a note of that one".

I then over flew Sevenoaks and performed my airfield approach checks and called for rejoin and landing instructions.

Very nervously I approached Biggin Hill. The boys said that I did a "Greaser of a landing". I think that must mean that I slid in well.

Fortunately for both the Examiner and myself all went well, I landed safely and walked away, which is why I can tell my story that at the age of 56 I became a

"PETTICOAT PILOT"

Champagne parties, many phone calls, flowers and presents came from far and wide. I was so proud and full of emotion it hurt.

I am now Captain Chance and a fully qualified danger to all who use the skies.

There are a number of reasons why I think it took me so long to learn.

I ran out of money once or twice, the weather was not good and not being able to fly every week is not often enough.

The main reason was, because in your fifties it seems to be harder to learn. The information goes in one ear, and then falls very rapidly out of the other one

PRIVATE PILOTS LICENCE

Certificate

This is to Certify that

ANN CHANCE

has successfully completed the C.A.A. syllabus and passed the Final Handling Test to qualify for the issue of a United Kingdom **PRIVATE PILOTS LICENCE.**

At BIGGIN HILL SCHOOL OF FLYING

On 10 MARCH 1993

Signed *A.H.Denyer* ANDY DENYER **Instructor**

London School of Flying
Denham School of Flying
Biggin Hill School of Flying
Blackbushe School of Flying
 BHSF BSF

LSF DSF

Since gaining my license I have taken a number of my disabled patients aloft and when airborne I let them take the controls if they want to. I usually point out a gasometer or something large and recommend they aim for that. Preferably up in the sky.

I have also taken many of my friends and all of my family on a trip of a lifetime.

They are still alive and most of them will still speak to me.

BLOODY *L*

...i PASSED!

Flying a light aircraft has its ups and downs in more ways than one. Many close encounters have taken place:-

I have experienced a brake failure on landing. I ran out of runway completely before I could finally make a stop. My passenger was very excited. It was a very comforting experience to have the fire crew alongside me as soon as I came to a halt. They did offer to give me a fireman's lift, which I declined this time. I'll take a rain check.

My rudder dropped off on landing, I think the string broke. What would have happened if it had fallen off in flight…who knows?

One day, whilst over flying the edge of Headcorn airfield, with their knowledge I hasten to add. Something glinted out of the corner of my eye. I threw the aircraft right hand down, and then saw an aircraft performing aerobatics. If I had not moved he would have come up underneath me and I would probably not be alive to tell this tale.

My last exciting adventure was to crash land on the runway. It was a very hot day, and the aircraft was happy in the air and did not want to come down. I tried twice, but I was not happy with my approach, so I aborted and went round again, twice.

This was costing me some money, which I could ill afford, so I made the stupid mistake and forced the plane down. It bounced on the runway, broke the nose wheel, which disappeared into the engine, and the propeller hit the runway twisting into a mass of unrecognisable metal and ground to a halt.

My favourite fire crew were there instantly. Fortunately I had remembered to switch everything off in case of fire. I was now hyperventilating and had difficulty in breathing. A fireman slapped my chest and said, "Big breaths".

Biggles

I don't remember that, but I was told that I actually said, "Yeth, and I'm only thixteen". With a lot of help I was lifted from the wreckage to discover that I could not walk. I was not injured physically, but my legs would not work. It was my ego that was a bit dented. I then broke down and sobbed which gave me the opportunity to receive a cuddle from every other pilot on duty.

When I had calmed down the debriefing took place. I admitted that it was pure pilot error, nothing else, engineered by money and stupidity. One hour later I was airborne again, to lay the ghost.

Every one in the control tower were talking to me and supporting me as I made my approach to land. Something I had done successfully many, many times before. I then

Wow! We've landed and live to tell the tale, myself and a son's friend from school

performed three go-a-rounds and a final landing, all safely. I was told that not many pilots get airborne again so soon after such a bad accident, but then I am not *many pilots*.

So beware, The Petticoat Pilot has been let loose at last.

I flew this 1942 Harvard also for my 60th Birthday present from my two sons

ACROSS AMERICA WITH A WHEELCHAIR

Since 1990 I have been a professional Senior Care Attendant looking after physically disabled clients, enabling them to remain at home with the family.

After performing the necessary care in the morning, I would drive many of them to their place of work.

Just to let them know that I cared, I would bring them home to the family at the end of the working day, so that in the morning I could repeat the process.

I was qualified to deal with tetraplegics, paraplegics and quadriplegics caused by road or sporting accidents, multiple sclerosis, rheumatoid arthritis, cerebral palsy and motor neurones disease.

My training has taught me some nursing skills, physiotherapy, moving and handling, food hygiene, health and safety and most important, how to have fun with people less physically fortunate than myself.

One of my clients, born with cerebral palsy lived very near to me, and as we are of a similar age group, became good friends.

In her younger days she not only went to work but also drove a car, but as the years progressed so did the disability.

One morning on my daily visit, let's call her Pat, was looking very down and shedding a few tears.

I did what all good friends do in this type of crisis I put the kettle on and made a cuppa.

I said, "Come on Pat, talk to me, and tell me what's wrong".

She replied, "Ann, sometimes life is a bummer and sucks".

Again I pushed the matter and said, "What's bothering you?"

She said, "Before I get too old and decrepit I have always dreamt of flying in a light aircraft into the Grand Canyon but I can't find an idiot to take me".

You know when you are going to open your mouth and put both feet right in, don't you? After at least a five minute discussion I agreed to be that idiot.

Many visits were made to the local travel agent, working out our routes, hotels with the correct facilities, and arranging for a large hire car to be at our first stop in Scottsdale, Arizona.

Pat visited her Doctor for a full check up, telling him what she was about to do and making sure that her medication needed, would last the journey.

We then spent the next six months planning what to do every day in America and what to visit en route.

Travel insurance was completed and accepted for us both, even though I declared that I was on more tablets than she.

A few weeks before our planned departure I received a phone call from my friends Doctor. I thought, something must be very wrong. The Doctor told me he had never known Pat to be so well, whatever I was doing, "Keep it up". "Have a great time and all at the surgery can't wait for your return to hear about the adventure."

My eldest son is an employee of Delta airlines, so through him I booked the flights.

I told him of our plans and asked him if he could arrange some excitement at Gatwick airport to make the beginning of our journey memorable.

I said, "Please don't tell me of your plans, I too would like to be surprised."

The taxi firm called Home James collected me on Wednesday, the day of departure, and drove a short distance to fetch Pat.

She was so excited I almost had to tie her down.

I physically lifted her into the front seat of the car and folded her mobile wheelchair into the boot. The driver put the suitcases on the back seats and we were off to Gatwick.

As the taxi drove up the slope at the airport we were met by a Delta rep. in full uniform, complete with clip board in hand, who then very deliberately in an affected efficient voice said, "On behalf of Delta airlines I would like to welcome you, Patricia, to Gatwick and hope that you have a fantastic holiday".

Pats' jaw noticeably dropped followed by a sideways look at me and said, "You must have something to do with this". Of course I denied all knowledge, knowing that I wouldn't be believed.

A porter got the wheelchair out of the boot, put it together and when ready I ceremoniously plonked Pat into a comfortable position, strapped her in and was about to start pushing when a Delta Rep took over this task.

The suitcases were placed on a waiting trolley; another porter took over this job leaving me to walk behind this entourage feeling like a celebrity.

Our tickets and passports were taken and we were checked through immigration and customs. Pat was frisked all over by a woman, not a man, and was found to be smuggling nothing. Wheelchairs are notorious hiding places for drugs, I was told. Pat enjoyed the attention and the search.

I walked through the metal detector and all was O.K. When I pushed Pat through all the bells from here to kingdom come began to ring.

The security guard grabbed me by the arm and looking at what I thought was my waist he said, "Its metal Madam". I quickly jumped to my defence and said, "Oh, come on it can't be metal my trouser belt is best Woolworth's' plastic". He then said in a very loud clear voice, "I actually meant the wheelchair Madam". We all had a damn good laugh when I at last realised he was taking me for a twit. After this fiasco we were then escorted into the V.I.P. lounge.

So this is what it's like to have money.

Fitted carpet throughout, piped music, fresh flowers and a number of very wealthy looking passengers.

Pat lives very frugally in a Council property, having only basic amenities, so this was an eye opener for her.

We were then served Champagne, caviar, toast, and very fancy tit bits.

My friend was in her best red and black N.H.S. wheelchair which somehow didn't fit in with the affluence of the lounge. Her electric wheelchair has to remain at home as it is too heavy to manhandle, doesn't fold and is impossible to get into a car.

VIP Lounge Gatwick

After sampling the fair, I needed to make a visit to the usual offices. I think it had something to do with all the excitement.

I told Pat where I was going and asked her if she would be O.K. for a while.

I have been into many toilets around the world but I have never seen anything quite so posh as those in the V.I.P. lounge at Gatwick.

Fresh flowers, music and marble worktops with fabulous stainless steel wash basins. The floor was so clean you could not only eat off it, but you could even prepare the food there if you had to.

Not a tap in sight just a spout. I wondered how I would wash. I placed my hand under the spout and would you believe it, the water began to run.

I was so thrilled I tried every spout in turn just for a bit of fun. I got so carried away that I forgot to do what I had gone in there to do.

I ran back outside to the lounge and told Pat, "You have to see this to believe it". I pushed her into the toilet area, where her face was a picture of disbelief. I thought that I could not let this moment pass without recording it for posterity. Pat was sitting in her wheelchair, (fully dressed) I hasten to add, I took a photo of her in the V.I.P. toilet. Just at that moment two very well dressed ladies entered, took one look at what I was doing and beat a very hasty retreat. They probably thought we were perverts of some sort.

All we did was laugh.

At last we were collected from the lounge and escorted to the aircraft a Boeing 777. One advantage to being in a wheelchair is that you are put on the plane first. When you land, you are taken off last. This isn't a problem as by the time you have to check out or collect your luggage, everyone else has gone and the only suitcases going around the turntable are probably yours.

I had pre-booked our seats in the centre of the aircraft, immediately behind the bulkhead of the first class area, so that nobody would be in front of us and Pat would have ample leg room. We were both seated and made comfortable before any other passengers were allowed to embark.

Take off was 30 minutes later than scheduled, fortunately not due to mechanical problems, but due to the fact that the cleaning brigade were late arriving.

At last the aircraft took off into the wild blue yonder and we both knew that our adventure was about to begin.

At precisely 10.35.a.m. G.M.T. the Captain said, "Please alter your watches as it is now only 6.30.a.m. Atlanta time".

We had three breakfasts, two lunches, one snack and lots to drink all at no charge.

The flight was to take 8 hours and 19 minutes, to be precise, which went fairly quickly, but it was quite a bit bumpy at 35,000 feet over the pond.

About half way across the Atlantic, Pat told me she needed to answer a call of nature. I rang the bell for the stewardess and told her that Pat needed to go to the toilet. She whispered, "You don't need permission to do that".

I very quickly replied, "Yes we do, Pat is disabled and cannot walk, you even helped me put her into her seat". I had been informed by the travel agent that this would not be a problem on this large aircraft.

The stewardess told us that as we were experiencing some heavy turbulence at the moment, it would be quite dangerous for all concerned to lift Pat from her seat, put her in a small wheelchair and navigate the length of the plane, which by now was tossing quite badly not only up and down but from side to side.

I was asked if my friend could wait. I nearly got cross here as I said, "Why don't you ask Pat that question, her brain works, it's only her legs that don't."

The Stewardess said she would speak to the Captain and come back with a reply as soon as possible.

After quite a bit more turbulence the stewardess came back and said that as it was now calmer it would be possible to go ahead with the tricky manoeuvre.

On asking why it was now so smooth, she said that she had felt very sorry for Pat and had discussed this matter with the Captain. I said, "Are you now saying that the Captain knows what Pat needs to do?" The reply was, "Yes, and so does the co-pilot".

Completely bemused now I asked her what was the next step?

She told me that our Captain had spoken to another aircraft at 37,000 feet and asked them what the weather was like up there. Their response was, "It's as smooth as a millpond up here do you have a problem?"

Our Captain then informed the other Captain that he had a disabled lady on board who needed to pay a visit, but at the moment there is too much turbulence to make it safe to go ahead. I asked the stewardess yet another question. "Are you telling us now that both Captain and co-pilot at 37,000 feet know what my friend wants to do?" She replied," Yes, isn't it exciting"

We were then informed that both Captains contacted Air Traffic control to ask permission to change places. So now everyone in the control tower knows what Pat wants to do. So the plane climbed 2,000 feet and the other aircraft came down 2,000 feet and the stewardess told us that we may now go.

I suggested that she get the airline wheelchair, as you remember, Pat cannot walk.

"Where is it?" the stewardess asked. I replied, "I don't know it's your chair and your airplane, not mine".

She offered to go and find it. Find it she did, underneath the seats of the passengers in First Class, who were now all asleep, curtains drawn and seats reclined. After some debate, the stewardess awoke all first class passengers, asked them to sit upright as a wheelchair was being sought, and could not be pushed through with the seats reclined. We both suddenly felt very popular.

Other people can perform this task without any fuss or anyone else knowing what is happening.

The wheelchair was at last found and Pat was ceremoniously put into it and wheeled from the front of the aircraft to the toilet at the rear.

Have you ever flown? Have you all used the loos on board the aircraft? How wide are the toilet doors? At least 15 inches I believe, not quite wide enough for a wheelchair. Both Pat and I struggled for some time to see if it would be possible to get her into the toilet. Pat can weight bear only if she has something to hold onto. I leaned over her and stood her up enabling her to hold onto the wash basin, but unfortunately I was still outside and couldn't perform the next manoeuvre. With a spark of an idea I climbed over Pat and stood on the back of the toilet to help my friend do what was necessary. Unfortunately, as I was now standing on the back of the toilet there was no way she could sit down. You won't believe how much I struggled to get her back into the wheelchair fully dressed, but not satisfied.

I spoke to the stewardess and said, "I was told that facilities were available for people like my friend". We were then informed that they usually are but the toilet for the disabled was, OUT OF ORDER.

I was trying to keep my cool as I asked the stewardess, "What do we do now?" Her reply was, "Let's try the first class toilets". Did you know one of the differences between first and tourist class is that the toilet doors are three inches wider. Money certainly talks.

I then pushed the airline wheelchair all the way from the rear of the aircraft to the front. Of course, by now, everyone on board knew what Pat was aiming to do. A few people even said, "Good Luck", as she passed by.

We made it to the front of the aircraft and the first class toilet. I have to say that the door was a little bit wider, but not much. At last, I got Pat where she needed to be, but the wheelchair was now stuck in the doorway, which I couldn't close. If any first class passengers had come by, they would have seen all.

One stewardess stood in the aisle to stop anyone visiting the toilets, whilst another got two blankets and folded them over the open door to give Pat the privacy she deserved. When she called for help I obliged, and after doing what I needed to do, Pat, at last, was now safely back in the wheelchair and ready to take her seat once again. As we arrived back in tourist class a number of passengers shouted congratulations.

Eventually back in our seats, I glanced at my watch. Forty-five minutes had lapsed from the time we left our seats, until we returned. But, long flights can be tedious, so at least this gave everyone something to concentrate on.

We had only been seated for less than five minutes when Pat decided to call the attendant again. I whispered, "I'm going to sort you out in a minute. We can't go through that again". Pat said, "Trust me". The stewardess asked Pat what she needed. She said, "Please send a personal message to both Captains, and co-pilots and all in the control tower thanking them very much. "One passenger is now very much relieved".

I knew this was going to be an adventure, I could feel it in my bones and we were only half way across the pond.

At precisely 2.05pm local time, 6.00pm G.M.T. we landed in Atlanta.

We checked our luggage and after a long wait we finally boarded a Boeing 747 at 4.30pm local time bound for Phoenix Arizona.

The air crew must have thought we were still hungry as more food and drink were served.

Pat told me that she didn't feel very well and by the colour of her face I knew she meant it. After calling for help and sick bags she was very ill. I put this down to too much food, air pressure and excitement, so I was not too worried.

She then started to experience what she described as severe stomach cramps.

I tried to straighten her body a bit to relieve the tension and gave her a pain killer. This pain stayed with her for the three hour flight. I was now getting very concerned.

During the flight I sat next to a Landowner from South Carolina who was on a World War II reunion, during which time he had served as a bomb aimer.

We arrived in Phoenix at 7.30pm Atlanta time, but as this is yet another time zone the clocks went back another two hours. Pat and I mused on the fact that we left Atlanta at 4.30pm flew for three hours and arrived in Phoenix just one hour later. Fiendishly clever these Americans.

The temperature was now 99 degrees. Very hot, to put it bluntly.

So far, we had spent the time going backwards through three separate time zones. We felt a little confused. One good piece of news Pat's pain had stopped.

With a lot of help from the carers at the airport we were taken to the underground car park, which was even hotter than the arrivals lounge, with no air to breath. Our brand new automatic car was there waiting for us.

I loaded the luggage and Pat, and prepared to drive away. This presented a small problem as I couldn't find the hand brake. I asked the porter who gave me the keys of the car but unfortunately as he was a Mexican he spoke no English and I do not speak Spanish apart from Ole. After much searching I was looking for something that didn't exist. The hand brake is incorporated in the gear shift. It seems that I have a lot to learn.

By this time I was very nervous, very tired and could not wait for the air conditioning to kick in to enable us both to cool off.

After driving around Phoenix at least three times plus a bit of help from the locals we finally made it to the Radisson Resort Hotel in Scottsdale, Arizona.

On checking in, there was no record of our booking. My name was on the ticket, but the hotels computer bore my friends' name. After what seemed a lifetime, we were taken to our room and just to show that I was friendly I tipped the porter a dollar.

What a fabulous room. Two king size beds very comfortable, a settee, table and chairs, a balcony, bathroom, fridge and coffee. Not bad eh?

We decided now at last to relax, unwind with a cup of coffee, a wash and then bed.

After a very good nights sleep we awoke refreshed and very hungry.

Pat lives very frugally at home so to see the menu for an American breakfast and what was available to her was mind blowing.

She had hash browns, a three egg omelette with mushrooms, ham and bacon. This was just the beginning. She followed with toast; marmalade and coffee add infinitum (whatever that means.) All I could manage was two eggs easy over with hash browns, bacon, sausage plus everything that Pat had.

We were entertained at breakfast by the waitress who loved to hear English people speak, and all of this at no extra charge.

Feeling very satisfied after that breakfast we decided to have a wander around the hotel and then to the local shops where we bought a sun hat for Pat and a few bottles of drink. This was most essential as the temperature was now 100 degrees. W O W!

Sitting by the pool relaxing we drank buckets of water and sweated even more. We decided this is the life we both liked.

After lunch we drove to Fountain Hills towards the picturesque Lake Saguaro, nestling in the mountains. Driving through the Mohave Desert, an Apache Indian Reservation, then the Salt River Reservation, the Union Hills and then on to Table Mountain at 2,805 feet high. What a sight.

Without any warning the heavens opened. There was thunder, lightning and flash floods which I was trying to drive through. The rain hit the desert sands and was forming rivulets of water cascading into the road. The water was so deep that I could only drive at about 3-5 miles per hour without getting into trouble. Pat was so excited, she said that it reminder her of a John Wayne movie. She might have been excited but that is not exactly what I was.

On arrival at the enormous lake, out came the sun and it was beautiful. Words could not do justice to what our eyes beheld. Sitting in the open by the lake we watched jet skiers having fun. Suddenly a road runner bird ran by, doing just what they do in cartoons, they run and boy do they run. There were even eagles soaring high on the thermals. Beautiful.

After liquid refreshments and an ice cream we headed back to the hotel. I have to own up here that I got slightly *mislaid* on the way back but arrived safely and in one piece.

Later, after a rest a wash and a change of clothes we drove to a town called Rawhide for a meal and an experience never to be forgotten.

Rawhide is a complete cowboy town set up as it would have been in the 1800's.

We not only met Wild Bill Hickock and Buffalo Bill but we shook hands with them both. Wild Bill took the wheelchair from me while the Sheriff locked me in the jail. Pat had to pay a dollar to get me out.

Pat decided to have a sepia photo taken in a costume of the era. This looked great and it is now framed and has pride of place on her lounge wall for all to see.

As our money was fast running out, I decided to go prospecting for gold. Having been taught how to pan I found quite a large lump which I gave to Pat.

As a special favour she will show you her gold teeth, for a small fee.

There then followed gunfights, stunts and a demonstration of dance by local Apache Indians. It was great fun and full of excitement.

All the local shops were open, including the jailhouse. As I knew what it looked like inside I gave the jail a wide berth.

The whole area was full of covered wagons, burros, horses and lots of action, including fight'n and shoot'n and cowboys falling off balconies and lying dead in the street below. Just like the movies again.

By now we were getting peckish so we went into the Rawhide saloon. The waiters were cowboys totin guns and wearing cowboy hats. We ordered a half rack of beef ribs, salad, corn on the cob, cowboy beans and spuds.

Pat followed this with a very large ice cream, but her eyes were bigger than her belly. Throughout the meal we were entertained by musicians playing true country and western music. A truly memorable experience.

Now full up, very happy but exhausted, we drove back to the hotel without getting lost this time. I must be improving.

The next morning, after yet another hearty breakfast, we were in the car and ready to go to Sedona. I did what the natives told me to do, I hung a right onto interstate highway north 17.

As we needed gas our first task was to find a filling station. I couldn't get the nozzle out of the pump, so I asked a lady who was filling her car, for some advice. To our surprise she was English, who came originally from London. We had a great chat and exchanged many stories.

Eventually I said, "How do you fill up here?" She replied "Here in

Arizona you pay the cashier first and then fill up". "According to how much gas you have put in, you either get a refund or pay a bit more". I think we should adopt this tactic in England.

Our next stop will be Sunset Vista which is a wonderful view point of the mountains. We were warned of snakes and scorpions, but they ignored us. After our comfort stop we picked up highway 17 again and would you believe, got stuck in a horrendous traffic jam. It brought back fond memories of England and the M25, only here it was hotter and higher.

We were now driving through the magnificent Prescott National forest, desert terrain and mountains finally reaching a height of 4,500 feet.

We navigated through Rock Springs, Black Canyon City, Black Hills Forest, Campe Verde an Indian Reservation and finally Montezuma National Monument and forest before coming upon Sedona at about 2.00.p.m.

After lunch and settling into our Hotel, we explored Uptown and Downtown.

The magnificent red mountains of Sedona have to be seen, the way they change colour as the day progresses is fabulous. I suffered dehydration after lunch and needed a little help. I think with the driving, the lifting of Pat in and out of the car and the Hotel, and finally pushing her wheelchair the length of Sedona high street in the heat of the day, taught me that there are boundaries to my capabilities. I think Sedona was trying to teach me a lesson as in the evening I was bitten by a very large black spider. My leg is better but the spider is not too well.

At 9.07 a.m. in beautiful sunshine, we left Sedona and headed towards the Grand Canyon with gnat bites, spider bites and happy memories. We travelled to Flagstaff, via Coconino National Forest, gaining in height from 5000 feet to 8050 feet. You can actually feel the difference in altitude.

The road then became very narrow as we drove along the windy route through the mountains, finally crossing a suspension bridge over Canyon Creek.

I thought I was carefully abiding by the State laws and stuck rigidly to just below the recommended speed limit of 40 m.p.h. Very soon I noticed a police car travelling behind us.

After some five minutes he flashed his lights, turned on the alarm and pulled us over. We were to be given a citation for travelling at 35 m.p.h in a 40 m.p.h. zone. As there were five cars behind us, according to the Sheriff of Sedona County, this is called impeding the movement of traffic. The Sheriff told me there would be no points on my license, no fine and I would not have to go to court, this was a warning. I have been *done* in England for exceeding the speed limit, but never for going slower than stated.

I had to produce my driving license and the hire care agreement. He wanted to know, where we were from, where we were going, was I tired, how tall was I, colour of my eyes, colour of my hair and my weight. I think given half the chance he would have liked to know what colour my knickers were, but I didn't tell him. It took him over 15 minutes to write the citation, and refused to let me get out of the car. The citation has been framed and is now hanging in Pat's toilet at home as a permanent reminder.

Unfortunately I was now getting angry, argumentative and finally upset when he said, "I hope I haven't spoilt your day". I replied, "You blooming well have". Pat took over at this point and calmed me down and when I felt ready I drove off at the required speed, followed by the Cops. He was still checking up on me.

After his car turned off the road, we were alone on the mountains. I put my foot down to see what speed our car could do. It reached 90.

Look out Flagstaff here we come.

One hour later, and more than six times around the one way system driving over railway lines and ignoring traffic lights, route 180 to the Grand Canyon was located. If anyone would like to know the ins and outs of this town, here are two very experienced travellers.

Places en route were the San Francisco Mountains and the Kaibab National Forest, where the highest point in Arizona is 12,670 feet above sea level.

Being very thirsty I pulled into a lay by to take a break and have a drink. There was another family there doing the same. They came from Essex. It's a small world.

Our second stop was called Sunset viewpoint in the Coconino National Forest.

As you can imagine the cameras were working overtime here.

Very soon we arrived at the Best Western Squire Inn, located next to a small airfield called Grand Canyon airways. This was situated near the South rim and Grand Canyon village. By now Pat is becoming uncontrollably excited.

ISSUE NUMBER	443953

ARIZONA DEPARTMENT OF PUBLIC SAFETY
☒WARNING ◯EQUIPMENT REPAIR ORDER
"COURTEOUS VIGILANCE"

SOCIAL SECURITY NUMBER (☐Same as DL #) — DRIVER'S LICENSE NUMBER **351108 A99 SM** — STATE / COUNTRY **ENGLAND** — CLASS

DRIVER: NAME: FIRST **ANN** — MIDDLE — LAST **CHANCE**

RESIDENTIAL ADDRESS **33 HOME FARM CLOSE** — CITY **BURGH HEATH** — STATE / COUNTRY **T** — ZIP CODE **78771**

SEX ☐M ☑F — WEIGHT **50T** — HEIGHT **PRN** — EYES **PRN** — HAIR **W** — ORIGIN — DATE BIRTH (MO/DAY/YR) **11/01/38** — RESTRICTIONS **—**

VEHICLE: COLOR **BRN** — YEAR **99** — MAKE **OLDS** — STY **DSD** — LICENSE PLATE **ADJ2625** — STATE / COUNTRY **CO.** — EXPIR DATE **700**

REGISTERED OWNER (☐ SAME AS DRIVER) **ALAMO RENTAL** — ADRESS **PHOENIX** — VEHICLE IDENTIFICATION NUMBER (VIN) **1G3NB52M1Y6342240**

OCCURRED: DATE (MO/DAY/YR) **9/25/99** — TIME OF DAY **0929** — SPEED **30** — APPROX **40** — POSTED — LOCATION **NORTHBOUND** — ON **89A** MP **383**

DRIVER SIGNATURE: X **A. Chance.**

OFFICER **G.A. HORN** — ID NUMBER/DISTRICT **5 6 0 3 1 2**

THE KEY TO SURVIVE - *DON'T* DRINK & DRIVE!!

☒ WARNING FOR VIOLATING

- ☐ EXPIRED REGISTRATION 28-302
- ☐ REGISTRATION NOT IN POSSESSION 28-305
- ☐ LICENSE PLATE POSITION / LEGIBILITY 28-309
- ☐ ATTACHMENT OF TAB 28-310
- ☐ TRANSFER OWNERSHIP 28-315
- ☐ LICENSE NOT IN POSSESSION 28-423
- ☐ CHANGE ADDRESS 28-427
- ☐ TRAFFIC CONTROL DEVICE 28-644
- ☐ SPEED 28-701/702
- ☒ IMPEDING TRAFFIC 28-704
- ☐ SLOWER TRAFFIC TO RIGHT 28-721
- ☐ LANE USAGE 28-729.1
- ☐ FOLLOWING DISTANCE 28-730
- ☐ IMPROPER TURN POSITION 28-751
- ☐ FAILURE TO SIGNAL LANE CHANGE 28-754
- ☐ LAMPS REQUIRED 28-922
- ☐ FAILURE TO DIM 28-942
- ☐ EYE PROTECTION 28-964
- ☐ OTHERS:

Note: This warning is issued to you as a courtesy and to remind you to do your part in promoting safety on our highways by closely observing our traffic laws.

◯ EQUIPMENT REPAIR ORDER

- ☐ HEADLAMP 28-924
- ☐ TAIL LAMP 28-925
- ☐ LICENSE PLATE LAMP 28-925.C
- ☐ STOP LAMP 28-927
- ☐ WHITE LIGHT TO REAR 28-931.C
- ☐ LAMP COLOR 28-939
- ☐ TURN SIGNAL 28-49
- ☐ BACK-UP LAMPS (forward motion) 28-940.C
- ☐ HEADLAMP COVER 28-941.4
- ☐ HEADLAMP ADJUSTMENT 28-949.C
- ☐ MUFFLER / SMOKE 28-955
- ☐ MIRROR 28-956
- ☐ WIPER / WINDSHIELD 28-957
- ☐ SPLASH GUARDS 28-958.01
- ☐ WINDOW TINT 28-959.01
- ☐ HANDLEBARS 28-964
- ☐ GAS CAP 28-965
- ☐ OTHERS:

NOTICE: A.R.S. 28-983.C states no person shall operate any vehicle after receiving a Repair Order except as may be necessary to return the vehicle to the residence or place of business of the owner or driver, within a distance of twenty miles, or to a garage, until the vehicle and its equipment has been placed in proper repair and adjustment and otherwise made to conform to the requirement of the statute.

If you have received a Repair Order, the Certification of Correction/ Adjustment of illegal or faulty equipment MUST be mailed to the Arizona Department of Public Safety, P.O. Box 6638, Phoenix, AZ 805-6638 Attn: Vehicle Equipment Repair within five (5) days.

Certification of Adjustment: I certify that the equipment on the motor vehicle described herein indicated has been tested and/or adjusted, and upon this date complies with the requirements of the motor vehicle laws of Arizona.

Firm Name: _____ Adress: _____

Signed by: _____ Date: _____

DISTRIBUTION: GREEN INK - DRIVER; BLACK INK - DPS — DPS 802-03330 Rev. 1/96

6548-0538-6407 ©1996, Mee® All Rights Reserved - 0305m

Arizona Police low speed citation

After a light lunch I booked a flight on a 15 seat aircraft, to finally carry out Pats' dream of a lifetime.

At the airport, everyone was so helpful including the Captain and co-pilot who physically lifted Pat on board, which was not easy as the plane was very small.

We lifted off at 3.00.p.m. for a 45 minute flight, travelling 100 miles in and around the Canyon. I almost feel that I should stop writing here as there are not enough words of the right calibre to describe the magnificent beauty and splendour of this *wonder of nature*.

Eventually back at our hotel, Pat experienced the cramp pain again and was sick.

We were now both a bit tired so after a light meal and some American T.V. we hit the sack. I think jet lag was catching up with us at last.

The next morning we arose at the crack of dawn, where even this early the temperature was still in the 90's. After breakfast we are going to the South Entrance of the Canyon. I pushed the wheelchair along the desert walk of

Grand Canyon, me & 'Pat'

the Canyon rim, where the temperature was soaring, so it was important to keep drinking to prevent dehydration.

After a rest and lunch I obtained a special permit to drive the entire length of the West Rim. All afternoon we were completely alone. Only coaches are normally allowed in this part of the Canyon which had finished running for the day, but as a disabled person some of the perks are worth having.

On the drive back to our Hotel, Pat fell asleep and she did not look well.

The next episode was very traumatic.

Back in our room I put Pat to bed, where she fell fast asleep. A few hours later when she awoke, she looked awful. She shouted at me for a bucket. I grabbed the only thing available which was the ice bucket into which she deposited two pints of blood.

I called for help and very rapidly. The paramedics arrived from the clinic situated in the Canyon. After a thorough examination, they found that she needed further treatment urgently. She was then taken in an ambulance 80 miles away to the big hospital in Flagstaff. The time was now 12.30.a.m.

On her arrival she was put on oxygen, a heart monitor, B.P. monitor, and a pulse rate monitor. In fact completely wired for sound. She needed a three pint blood transfusion. Pat was in safe hands. I was then collected from the Clinic in the Canyon at 2.00.a.m.

The next morning after a fitful night I left the Grand Canyon alone. After packing all the cases, and settling the hotel bill I drove back to Flagstaff to try to find the hospital.

Pat was in the critical care unit of this fabulous hospital, awaiting an endoscopy examination, plus an all over body scan to determine if there were any blood clots. The answer to that was in the negative, I'm glad to say.

With the help of the Doctor, I booked into a hotel called Fairfield Inn in Flagstaff. Being very familiar with the one way system I was becoming highly efficient at finding my way around.

After the endoscopy the Doctors found the cause of the problem which was four ulcers in the oesophagus. These had burst, causing the pain and severe bleeding. The ulcers had been cauterised and Pat was be transferred to a ward in the morning.

Finally in my room at the Hotel I was very upset, I thought the holiday would be at an end. To cheer myself up, I ate all Pats' toffees, watched wrestling on the telly then went to bed.

After a good nights rest and breakfast, I telephoned the hospital to discover that Pat would be discharged by lunchtime. She was fit and well and raring to go.

I settled the hotel bill, packed all the bags, loaded the car, drove

Disabled lady in power boat on Lake Powell

around Flagstaff once again, just for old time's sake and finally made it to the hospital.

A carer helped me give Pat a shower, wash her hair, put all clean clothes on. She looked and felt like a million dollars when we had finished.

After having lunch in the hospital, with the help of the doctors and nurses we were escorted to the car park, where we said our fond farewells. We both felt good at this point. We had only missed one stop, Monument valley. A small price to pay for good health. What a good job we had taken out full medical cover insurance. The final bill, which we didn't pay, was just over $4,000.

The journey from Flagstaff to Page was indescribable and spectacular. Driving up mountain passes, through mountain cuts and gorges, across deserts and finally through the Navaho Indian Reservation. We even saw one Indian. En route we visited Sunset Crater National Monument, Hopi Indian Reservation, Wupatki National Monument, Cedar Ridge, Echo Cliffs, culminating in the Navajo bridge over the Colorado River. This bridge has mind blowing dimensions. It is 467 feet above the river and 616 feet long over Marble Canyon.

By this time we were running low on gas, but luckily we found a station in the middle of the desert and filled up a very thirsty car.

Lake Powell came into view at about 5.00.p.m. The name of the Hotel was Wahweep Lodge which in Indian means 'bitter water'. The Canyon which had been flooded to build a dam belonged to the Indians, hence, 'Bitter Water'.

The scenery here was vast, magnificent and tranquil. It was now time for a cup of tea which we drank whilst sitting on our balcony watching the sun sink slowly in the west.

After a well earned rest and a wash we went to a posh restaurant to celebrate Pats' good health and recovery and my *simply wonderful driving skills* at not getting lost once from Flagstaff to Lake Powell.

Very tired, but satisfied we hit the sack early.

Whilst we were getting ready to leave for Bryce Canyon I noticed a sign saying, "Power boat rides into the Canyon". I enquired if it would be possible to lift my disabled friend on board. The crew replied, "No problem Ma'am". Pat was lifted on board and placed at the stern with due ceremony. This was as far as she could go with a wheelchair. Much to the dismay of some passengers, (mostly men) the pilot was a young woman. The speed varied from very fast to a slow creep. We navigated through a very narrow gorge with only feet to spare on either side.

We were shown a group of rocks called Indian Tapestry. The lines in the rocks had been caused by chemicals seeping through, which gave the appearance of a curtain. To get out of this gorge, a very clever three point turn was manoeuvred, *very slowly* and then when the water got deeper we drove at very high speed for nearly an hour.

The Dam was the next stop. It is so large you cannot help but feel vulnerable. Remarkably the sky and the water were azure blue.

Almost completely speechless we packed the car and took the scenic byway to Kanab en route to Bryce Canyon.

We drove through Smokey Mountain, Glen Canyon (now in Utah) through Vermillion cliffs, Pink Mountains and White Cliff Mountains, which were surrounded by pink sand dunes.

Being now at 7,000 feet we were really beginning to notice the change in height. There were Canyons, dry river beds, washes and creeks. It is to me what America has always been, desolate and beautiful. Like the films or books I used to read as a kid.

Kanab is a small American West town, full of cowboys and Indians. So to keep up with tradition we had lunch at McDonalds. No choice, it was the only place to eat, plus very good facilities for wheelchair users.

To keep us entertained during this time, we watched a lady drive a truck into a ditch. Cowboy language is very colourful. It was 30 minutes before a tow truck was found to pull her out. Everyone in McDonalds, including us, took their lunch outside to watch, and help with suitable suggestions, all of which were ignored.

When the excitement had died down we made our way to Mount Carmel Junction and eventually to Red Canyon and then into Bryce Canyon National Park, where without too much trouble we located the Great Western Ruby Inn.

Another time change took place here. One hour forward as we were now in Utah and not in Arizona. Our room was on the ground floor in a block of Lodges with our individual parking space overlooking a very large lake. After a large meal, we retired very happy and looking forward to our day in Bryce Canyon.

Up at the crack of dawn and on to the restaurant where we devoured a very large breakfast as the mountain air really made us hungry. Much refreshed we were in the old Wild and Woolly Western Town, stepping back in time.

The Town was made of timber with a wooden "pavement" and a rail where your "Hos" could be tethered. Pat locked me in the jail and if she pays the fine on time I will be out soon. I bought my first ever cowboy hat here and a Daniel Boone racoon hat for my Grandson.

After lunch we toured the hotel just to find everything then sat in the sunshine by the lake opposite our room. I could grow to like this lifestyle given half a chance.

On our walkabouts I noticed a Helicopter pad offering flights into the Canyon.

I secretly enquired if it would be possible to lift a disabled person on board. The usual reply was, "No probs Ma'am leave it to us".

Getting Pat into the helicopter was more difficult than I had envisaged, but the Captain and one member of staff from the hotel obliged. We were the only two people on board, apart from the Captain that is, and we flew for 35 minutes into a magical wonderland of extreme vastness colour and beauty. Our photos do not do the trip justice; it has to be experienced to take it all in. There were Macers, Butes and Hoodoos. These are all the different shapes of the worn rocks in the Canyon which are red/brown in colour.

Attacked by Indians

The pilot then flew us into the Rainbow Amphitheatre below the level of the ridge. Wow! At this point we both screamed with excitement and exhilaration. What a flight and what a memorable time for Pat. Her face was a picture.

All too soon we flew back to the Heli pad where Pat was unloaded. I fell out and almost in silence we made our way back to the Inn.

After a restful afternoon by the lake, we made yet another big decision.

This was to ride in a covered wagon on a cowboy cookout. Yet again I had to make sure that it would be possible to get Pat on board. There were three steps up into the wagon and the first one was a long way off the ground. With the Americans usual "Joie de vie", this task was completed, but not without some danger to Pat. With every ones help, Pat and the other eleven people were now safely on board. The Lady Cowgirl called Alice was our guide. Her Great Grandparents were some of the first settlers to found Utah. Her Great Grandfather had been captured by Indians, tortured and fortunately released, much to the delight of Alice. If this had not been so, she would not have been born. She introduced us to the Mexican teamster, "The Best in the West" in charge of two large Shire type horses.

Hanging on the back of the wagon next to my nose were many animal pellets, which we might need to trade with the Indians! A Mountain man on horseback escorted the wagon. He was dressed in a full hide outfit, with a dead coyote hat and a double-barrelled shot gun. His words, "Just to keep you safe from Indian attack". His name was Yasmo and we had to practice calling his name very loudly in case the Indians should attack.

Some five minutes later four or five fully dressed and war painted Crow Indians on horseback came screaming out of the woods and attacked our wagon. It was terrifying, but it made us realise what it must have been like some 100 years ago. Their screams and whoops were so authentic. Their speed on horseback and the way they suddenly changed direction left us all buried in a cloud of dust and the Indians were no longer visible. It was definitely clean underwear time. The Indians had captured Yasmo, tied him to a pole on a hillside and wished to parley.

Two men from our wagon had to disguise themselves in poke bonnets, petticoats and skirts, one of which had to be red, as the Indians are very partial to that colour. Bartering took place and eventually the Indians accepted all the animal pellets in exchange for Yasmo. We in turn were given presents of spears adorned with feathers and scalps.

It was all so authentic we almost began to believe it.

During the battle we could hear many shots being fired but because Yasmo ran out of ammo, that is why he was captured. Or so we were told.

The wagon then drove on through the burial grounds. The graves were on the hillside with all the trappings.

Peace had finally been made with the Crow Indians. Unfortunately we did not possess a pipe of peace but, we were taught how to scream very loudly to frighten off the Indians should they try to attack again. Luckily for us they saw sense and left us alone.

Arriving at a very large tepee we experienced a Wild West cook out of chicken, corn, beans, hash browns, fruit, jelly and coffee.

After satisfying our appetites we cleared away the food and the benches to the edges of the tepee, ready for the next bit of fun, a country and western ho' down with live music. All the musicians were family members of Alice and Yasmo, ranging from very young to more mature. It was FABULOUS.

We were all singing and dancing apart from Pat, who could not take part in the eight some reel.

With help from everyone, I pushed the wheelchair so that Pat and I were as one. I had to strap her in very tightly as the chair from time to time tipped up on one wheel. Hard work for me, but satisfying enough to see Pat singing, dancing, and having a ball.

The finale of the evening was a small grandson of five years old riding into the tepee on a quarter horse carrying the American flag. We all stood to attention whilst the anthem was sung. Not a dry eye in the tepee. It was very moving and a wonderful end to a great experience.

The next bit was also fun as we then had to get Pat back on to the covered wagon. This had to be seen to be believed but in the end was a great success.

On our drive back through the forest and the Indian Territory in the cold and dark it was obligatory to sing cowboy songs as loudly as we could to frighten the Indians. I think the noise we made would have frightened anyone.

Back at the Hotel, the next difficult task was to get Pat off the wagon. So to speak. Before I could give instructions, a very large South African gentleman decided that he could perform this task alone. He picked her up like a baby cradling her in his arms and proceeded to walk backwards down the three very small wooden steps to the ground. I screamed for assistance as I saw him lose his footing as he couldn't see where he was putting his feet.

Three of us rushed to help and we all put our hands on this very large South African bottom and steered him safely with Pat to the ground. I've never had my hands in that position before, but there's always a first time.

We said our heartfelt thanks to one and all and went to bed frozen solid but very happy.

At 10.15.a.m. we left Bryce Canyon, but we didn't really want to, our time here had been wonderfully memorable.

We decided to 'hang a right' out of the Hotel and then made our way to Highway 63, 12 and 9 on to the Scenic Byway, heading for Zion National Park.

What a sight! Not only were the hills and mountains reddish brown but the road had been made to match. The fee to drive through the park was 10 dollars. The best 10 dollars we had ever spent. This was a magnificent drive through tunnels, mountain arches and narrow winding roads, which really tried my driving skills. The rock formations looked like melted toffee, caused by past volcanic action.

The next town we came across was called Virgin, then Dixie National Forest, the Virgin Mountains and then back into Arizona.

Then we made our way to Nevada and the town of Mesquite, the Valley of Fire and the Virgin River. After driving through the Moapa River Indian Reservation we finally hit the Nevada desert. We were now about 300 miles from our destination; Las Vegas.

The small hick towns with wooden houses and stoops, or verandas to us British, was like turning back the clock, and something I had only ever seen in the movies.

It was now very hot, dry and dusty and due to the many mirages I was seeing the road looked as if it was under water.

The visibility was now very poor due to the heat and my eyesight was beginning to suffer. Pat found my sunglasses and said, "Don't worry if you can't see just keep your nose straight, there is only one road". Sometimes it pays to have a sense of humour.

As we approached Las Vegas I became more and more nervous as the traffic was horrendous. If you know where you are going this is not a problem. We didn't get lost though, we were just temporarily uncertain of our position.

Eventually we located the Flamingo Hilton, with, I hasten to add, help from the locals. The hotel was enormous, noisy, brash and typically American with gambling 24 hours a day, seven days a week, and 365 days a year.

The room we were given was not suitable for wheelchair access. Getting Pat into the bathroom was a major expedition. I now have muscles where muscles do not normally exist.

At Pat's suggestion we ordered supper to be served in our room. This arrived complete with waiter and cloth covered table. Again, just like the movies. We even looked under the cloth to see if a gangster was hiding there. After supper we pushed the table outside our room and hoped that someone would fetch it and wash up.

My first job in the morning was to return the car to Alamo at Vegas airport. I was not prepared to do any more driving. No more damage was going to be inflicted on my nervous system.

After breakfast we strolled through the Flamingo Hilton gardens, seeing all the wild life, six swimming pools, enormous carp in the lakes, real Flamingos, ducks, swans and would you believe real live penguins. They must have felt a bit hot as the temperature was 100 degrees.

A white wedding was taking place in the chapel, situated in the grounds of the hotel. This was yet another dream come true for Pat. The groom must have been melting as he was dressed in black tuxedo and

Mount Rushmore

bow tie. I nearly forgot, black trousers as well. I expect he couldn't wait to get into something cooler.

Now it was time to help Pat with another dream, to visit a night club. I booked tickets for a Las Vegas show at the Riviera Hotel, called *Splash*. I also found a lady taxi driver whose speciality was transport for the disabled. Her van was equipped with a tail lift. A relief for me and Pat as it meant no more heavy moving from wheelchair to vehicle and back again.

The show was good, clever, and noisy with interesting water effects and lots of topless swimmers. Perhaps that is why it was called *Splash*. We enjoyed it.

After the show, our taxi arrived driven by Charlie, who had such a slow drawl, we did not understand a word he said. So we laughed and said "Yes" or "No" at suitable times.

The next day we decided to be lazy and after a late brunch by the pool, we wrote our diary whilst cooking gently in the 99 degree heat.

This was our last day in America. We had a wonderful two weeks with only a few minor hiccups along the way.

At 7.00.a.m. the next morning we arranged a taxi to take us to Las Vegas airport all of three miles away up the road towards the desert.

We were trying to get ourselves in gear ready for the long journey home where it will be considerably colder and one day short of a week.

After a rest and a wash we changed into something posh and ate in the splendid Flamingo dining room. It was our last night so we thought we would spend some money and live like millionaires for the evening.

We had one attempt at the gambling casino on a one armed bandit. We lost a whole dollar, so decided to save our money.

After dinner I pushed the wheelchair for two hours up and down the entire length of the strip. This for me was exhausting, but for Pat, it was awe inspiring.

On Monday we sadly vacated our room and left the Flamingo Hotel for Vegas airport.

The plane left Vegas at 9.00.a.m. but in Atlanta it was already 12.30 p.m. Is it breakfast or lunch time? On the three hour flight to Atlanta we had brunch.

Whilst waiting for our connection flight to Gatwick, I suggested that Pat make a visit to the toilet, as I could not go through the procedure again as we had done on the outward journey.

In the confusion of heat and exhaustion I left her bum bag in the toilet containing all her worldly goods. On trying to check in, I asked Pat for her passport. That is when I realised what I had done. I didn't know I could still run that fast. The bag was not there.

On arriving back at check in, the desk clerk was waving the bag in front of me. Another lady with disabilities had followed us into the toilet, seen the bag and handed it in. Saved again.

We boarded the plane in Atlanta at 6.00.p.m. local time where now in England it was only 1.00.a.m. On the seven hour flight home we had lunch, dinner and breakfast. Fortunately for all concerned Pat did not need to visit the usual offices. We arrived at Gatwick at 7.10.a.m. and we were driven home to chilly Surrey.

Is today Monday or Tuesday, day or night? We don't really care.

We had come to the end of a near perfect two weeks in America.

SADDLE SORE IN MONTANA

To be a successful wrangler it is important that you learn how to yell out "Yi Ha! Head 'em up, Move 'em out and Wagons Roll". So by all means before reading any further perhaps you would like to practise this a few times to get you in the right frame of mind.

Plans for my next adventure started on my eighth birthday, but it didn't take place until I was 63, so you can tell from this snippet of information, I am the sort of person who likes to get things done in a hurry.

On my eighth birthday, my Dad bought me a Buffalo Bill Annual which, would you believe, introduced me to Buffalo Bill, Wild Bill Hickock, Jesse James, the Hole in the Wall Gang, plus stories of the wild and woolly west.

From that day to this I have always wanted to be a cowboy, not a cowgirl. My dream was to be able to ride the range with a couple of good looking Wranglers either side of me, yell out, "head 'em up", dress like a cowboy and round up cattle.

At the end of a very long day in the saddle, to come back to camp, and sit on a bale of hay round the camp fire, with the good looking Wrangler. We would play my guitar, watch the shooting stars overhead and the piece de resistance, to eat baked beans. I have now learnt why they eat them in the open.

What must it be like to live under canvas, or the stars, and not to wash for a whole week.

I, as a child never thought this could happen. Fortunately I was wrong.

I decided to get fit and learn to ride, at least English style for the moment. I made a weekly visit to the gym, where I finally lost 12 pounds in weight, whilst at the same time strengthening my leg muscles.

As I live very near Epsom Grandstand, finding a riding stable was not a problem. I telephoned my designated school and asked for some private riding lessons. The young man enquired, "Why private?" I told him that as I thought I would make a fool of myself I would like to do it on a one to one basis.

My next request was to be taught by a young good looking man not a woman. He told me he was the chief riding instructor and volunteered to take on this massive task.

On arrival at the school, a young man was sitting at the desk. He very politely said, "Good Morning, how can I help you?" I said, "I am the lady who booked some private riding lessons". He looked me up and down and said, "Can I ask how old you are?" I replied, "64 why?" He said, "Well, I don't want to be nosy, but why have you left it this late before learning to ride?"

I said, "I am taking part in my first cattle drive in the Montana badlands in ten months time". He replied, "I think we had better get cracking".

After some preliminary instruction I was taken outside to where a horse was saddled and waiting for me to mount. Getting onto a horse in a riding stable is not difficult, because you are standing higher than it. Without any struggle I was now astride and raring to go.

We then made our way to the outside sand arena. The instructor asked me if I had ever ridden before. When my two sons were smaller, and wanted to have riding lessons, once or twice I sat on a horse and walked it up and down the high street. I can assure you that this bears no resemblance to rounding up cattle in Montana.

He then asked me if I knew what made the horse move forward. All I could remember was that if you said "Chck. Chck", in theory it should move. He told me that would do for the moment.

"Do you know how to trot?" he asked. I replied that all I knew was that every so often you had to raise your bottom off the horse. I never got it right. When the horses' bottom went up, mine went down. This is quite painful after a short period of time. He said, "Trust me". "You'll get it right eventually".

I asked if there was a secret to the timing. I was told that if you watch the horses' left shoulder, when that goes back your bottom goes up.

Now, I am not normally one to make trouble, but it has been some 35 years since I sat on a horse. I was a mature woman of 64 and he wanted me to hang over the side of the horse, watch its' left shoulder go back and at the same time try to rise up and down in a correct sequence.

During the first hour, I walked the horse around the arena, and was told that I had a lovely seat. I didn't know what that meant, but it sounded like a compliment. During this time, once or twice I tried to trot and for a few seconds, got it right.

My instructor thought that after an hour in the saddle we should call it a day. I have to be honest; I was delighted at this request.

On arrival back at the dismounting area, he told me that I could now get off. I said, "How do you do that?" He said, "Take both feet out of the stirrups, throw your right leg nonchalantly over the back of the horse and slowly lower yourself to the ground".

Now when you're 64 and you haven't sat in that position for some time with a large beast between your legs, there are parts of your body that cease to function. Every time I tried to throw my leg over, I suffered severe cramp in my groins and my calves. I replied that I couldn't get off. I was told, "Wait there, I'll go and get help". Where did he think I was going?

Eventually the instructor returned with another young man to help solve the problem. One put his hands on my bottom whilst the other one grabbed my right leg and threw it off the horse. I was now on the ground, but unfortunately my legs were still in the same position as they were whilst on the horse. It took some time before I could get my legs together again. It would have been impossible to drive the car home with your legs at such a strange angle.

During the next few weeks I improved and eventually learnt how to trot, even getting the sequence right most times. I learnt how to move the critter forwards and backwards plus a small amount of dressage, to help me gain control of not only the horse but myself as well.

One sunny Wednesday morning I arrived yet again for another lesson. The instructor told me that, "Today Ann, I am going to teach you how to C.A.N.T.E.R.". I said, "Why on earth don't you just say Canter?" At this point the horse took off at speed with me on board. I screamed, "Do something". Of course without any help from me the horse was brought under control. "Why on earth did you spell C A N T E R", I whispered. His answer was a gem. He said that the horse was quite smart but fortunately couldn't spell. Another lesson learnt very quickly.

After a few more lessons, I was beginning to feel more confident, or so I thought. The day dawned bright and sunny and on arrival at the riding school my instructor said, "Today Ann, I am going to take you out of the school for a ride over the Downs".

The two of us saddled up and made our way to my first trot and canter out of the safety of the school. Trotting along a very narrow bridleway, my teacher said, "Are you ready for some C.A.N.T.E.R?" I said, "Don't bother to spell it, just say it, I can cope".

We proceeded along at quite a good lick, it was very exhilarating. If not for the tight fitting hard hat, the wind would have been blowing through my hair. Suddenly we cantered past what looked like a broken blue bucket.

Now, my horse not only disliked blue, but disliked buckets and he decided to stop. This is not normally a problem, but he did not discuss this matter with me first, and he put all his brakes on.

I immediately lost my left stirrup and the metal ground itself into my calf, paralysing my leg and giving me a bruise which was still visible some four years later. Luckily I was still on the horse, but I was not in the saddle. I was sitting on the horses' neck, whispering in his ear. Due to the fact that I have lost one stirrup I am slowly falling off to one side. Boy, it's a long way down. I screamed at my instructor to come back and help me. He turned his horse and cantered back to my aid. He said, "On the count of three, push down hard into the one stirrup you have left, I will grab the front of your clothes and hoist you back into the saddle". On the count of three I pushed hard into the stirrup, he grabbed me, threw me back into the saddle and ripped all my clothes down the front of my coat.

On getting back to the stables, the girls all seeing my dishevelled appearance said, "What happened to you"? I said, "It was my instructor you know, he took advantage of a poor defenceless woman whilst riding over the Downs".

A few more weeks went by and the time was nearing my departure to Montana. On arrival at the stables I was told by my instructor, "today Ann you are going over the Downs without me but with a group of very experienced riders. This is the time to do your first gallop."

You know when something exciting is going to happen as the hair on your neck begins to bristle. I knew that the horse was ready, but was I?

After saddling up and some final words of encouragement we set off. Due to all the new safety regulations there are very few places that one is allowed to gallop, unless you are an expensive race horse. The place in question is called Mitchell's' Gallop.

As we got nearer, the horse knew where he was going. His ears started to twitch, his nostrils flared, and all four legs were stamping with impatience. I was asked if I was ready. I told the group that I wasn't but the horse was.

We started with a trot, then a canter, and finally into my first gallop. I find it hard to describe this feeling. It is frightening, exciting and a completely new experience. I screamed to let them know I was alright, but asked how to make the horse slow down. They all said, "Don't worry, we are going up hill and when we get to the top the horse is so exhausted he will automatically slow down". I'm glad to say that he did just that.

On that day we were riding for two hours, which was already one hour longer than I had ever been in the saddle. On arrival back at the school, I was asked if I was alright and if I could get off alone without any help. It's nice to be looked after like this. We senior citizens need to be spoilt from time to time. I told the riders that as I was now highly skilled I could manage thank you.

I took both feet out of the stirrups, threw my right leg nonchalantly off the horse. I always hold the cantle part of the saddle during this manoeuvre to help lower me to the ground as I have a very severe arthritic right knee. I was lowering myself with my chest against the flank of the horse. When I got to within a foot of the ground I could suddenly go no further. I was hanging on the side of the horse. I was too far down to get back up again and I was too high up to reach the stirrups to get back on again.

The riders laughed and said, "Stop hanging about Ann and get off". I said, "I can't, I'm hanging".

What had happened was that one of the saddle buckles had come undone and as I lowered myself the hook dug into my clothes, lodged there, and I could not get off. I asked for someone to hold the horse as I felt that if he decided to bolt with me hanging on his side, this could be a problem. One rider kindly obliged while the others went off to get the help urgently needed. Three young men came back including my instructor and stood there discussing me and my problem as if I didn't exist. Two of the young men placed their hands on my bottom to push me up higher, whilst my instructor had to put his hands into my clothing to release the offending object. He does know me now quite intimately. On a good day his wife will even speak to me.

All of my clothing including my jodhpurs, my knickers and my long johns were now in shreds, revealing quite a lot to all that were watching. Everyone laughed at such a spectacle. The stable talked about it for a long time and it is one of those things that is remembered with fondness.

After having parted from my horse on more than one occasion, everyone thought that I had now learnt enough to at least take part in my first cattle drive.

I spent the next few months acquiring the correct clothes for this adventure. Wrangler jeans and a cowboy hat, complete with stampede strap were first on my list. I bought some cowboy boots from a Gaucho Store in Madrid. It is important that the boots are 18 inches tall, as Rattle snakes don't strike any higher than 18 inches, it says in the book. I think mine are only 17 inches tall, but they have kept me alive so far. Long sleeved shirts are a must, a bandana or two and a real live 'slicker'. Plenty of cream is required, to rub in certain places when necessary. A rucksack, sun tan lotion, a cantle bag, saddle bags to the uninitiated, and clean knickers.

On August the 5th of 2001 I left Gatwick Airport at 12.10pm on a DC10 for the first leg of my journey to Minneapolis, Montana. When the plane landed I was getting tired, my body clock said it was now 9pm but only lunchtime in Montana. Should I have lunch or evening meal? The temperature was 102°. Phew.

An hour later I boarded another plane for a 2 hour flight to Bozeman.

This is known as Big Sky Country. I later found out what this meant.

We landed at 7.30pm local time, but as I had crossed another time zone, it was 1.00am to me. Should I have dinner or go to bed? Life can be confusing, can't it? I used the free courtesy phone in the airport to arrange to be picked up and taken to the Best Western Gran Tree Inn for my first overnight stop. I was very hungry and made my way to the restaurant. According to my body the time was now 3.00am so I ate heartily and fell into bed at 9.30pm American time, 4.00am my time. I was exhausted.

The hotel and the room were great with every facility, including a heated indoor pool. I could see I was going to enjoy this trip.

At 5.00am I was wide awake, sitting up in bed, drinking buckets of coffee, writing my diary and doing a crossword.

At 8.00am my alarm call came through and after breakfast I arranged to be collected and taken to the ranch, ready for the adventure.

In Montana, Manyana is very apt. I was not collected from the Hotel until 12.30. The temperature was a mere 96°. We spent the afternoon sitting in a very hot vehicle, picking up other visitors from the airport and going shopping. We then changed vehicles and transferred to a Suburban. I thought that was where you lived not a vehicle. We were then driven over the mountains to the campsite.

To say that the facilities at the camp site were basic, is putting it mildly. The tents were not erected, there was very long grass, full of weeds, grass hoppers and I was a bit frightened to think what else there might be in the undergrowth.

During the late afternoon we introduced ourselves to everyone plus the horses and wandered aimlessly, not really knowing what to do or where to go. I began to question what I had let myself in for.

Finally the chuck wagon served dinner under the stars. After chow we collected our sleeping bags and foam mattresses and got dressed for bed. Please note dressed for bed not undressed, it was very cold in the mountains at night. We had no pillows so we all used our rucksacks. I paid for this privilege. There were six of us in this big tent. Canvas strung over wooden poles to be precise, not even fixed to the ground in many places.

Our first breakfast was eggs easy over, bacon, hash browns, fruit juice and good ol' Cowboy coffee all served in the open at 7.30am, sitting on bales of hay around a camp fire. We were then given a lesson on how to ride Western style plus how to round up cattle.

The wranglers then assigned us our horses, according to the

My bedroom

qualifications we had submitted earlier. Mine was called Houdini. It didn't take me long to discover how he acquired this handle. He was never where I left him. Whichever knot I tied, he managed to somehow get it undone.

After lunch of a hamburger and hot dogs, we were off for a short trail ride just to experience the wide open spaces. If we found some cattle, we were given the opportunity to practise what to do with them. We saddled up and began a three hour ride. This was already 1 hour longer than I had ever been in the saddle in England.

We rode through the burnt forest and just like the movies we rode through the sage brush. The smell that came up was very strong. All I wanted then was the chicken and the onions.

On arrival back at the camp, we enjoyed a well earned rest. At 7.00pm the cook rang the big metal triangle to announce that it was now chow time.

I was sitting on a bale of hay around a camp fire, surrounded by good looking wranglers, one of whom was strumming gently on his guitar. There were shooting stars overhead. The evening meal consisted of rack of beef, pork ribs and chicken. Guess what else was served. Yes, you're right, Baked Beans.

Suddenly all my dreams were coming true. This was more than I could handle and I started to have a few tears. My wrangler noticed this and said, "What's the matter Annie?" I replied, "I'm so bloody happy". He felt very sorry for me and said, "Come here Annie, I'll give you a cuddle".

Suddenly all the other wranglers saw this and said, "What's he got that we haven't?" I replied, "If you all care to form a straight line I will work my way along and cuddle you all in turn". I thought, play your cards right Ann, and if I get a bit emotional every evening, it could be fun.

Just before we all went off to bed the chief wrangler informed us that he was the tick inspector. He told us that the cattle have got ticks and so have the horses. Before the week is out we might also get a tick or two. He said, "We now have to be up every morning at 5.15am getting the cattle moving before the heat of the day comes down".

We were shocked by this, not only by the time, but what on earth is a tick call?

He told us that at 5.15am the next morning, he would knock on our tent and yell out "Tick Inspection".

"So what happens next?" I asked. He replied, "Well, I come into your tent yelling 'Tick Inspection' and get into your sleeping bag with you, rip all your clothes off and check your body all over for ticks". "I've got news for you, there are six of us in this tent and it is so cold at night in the mountains, that by the time you have stripped me of all my layers of clothing, it will be the end of the week". I answered.

When 5.15am came, and the tick inspector arrived, we all threw our boots at him. He disappeared rather rapidly.

In the morning whilst still in my sleeping bag, which was covered in dew, I took off all the night layers of clothing and dressed in the true traditional cowboy outfit ready for my first round up. We had to get dressed first and only wash what's left showing with very handy wet wipes. I then walked over to the one basin on a stand and cleaned my teeth and then used the portaloo. The temperature was still very cold.

After filling my cantle bags or saddle bags with sun tan lotion for later, anti-midge spray, toilet paper and water, we saddled up and were out on the range by 7am. I could not believe that I was really going to do this.

We rode through canyons, draws and mountains, looking for strays. We stopped in a clearing in the woods where the chuck wagon found us and supplied a very basic lunch. We hit the trail again and finally rounded up 150 head of cows, calves and bulls.

To ride behind that number of cattle all mooing, the horses whinnying, and the dogs who were helping us constantly barking at the heels of the cattle, is just like any western you have ever seen. As if this was not noisy enough then there was the noise of all of us. We were yelling 'Yi ha',

'Head 'em up', 'Move 'em out'. The wranglers were yelling 'Wi Wi', which we copied at first very quietly, then as we became braver we too began to yell aloud. When the wranglers then yelled in a very loud voice, 'Move yer arses you silly damn cows, git back inta the herd', I suddenly felt at home and verbally joined in with great gusto.

That day we were seven hours in the saddle, with only two stops for a rest, drinks, eats and toilet breaks in the woods. During the day I had been asked to ride drag. This was at the rear of the herd making sure that the cattle keep moving forward and that they do not run backwards in the direction of where they had been earlier.

Suddenly the calf just in front of me turned and ran in the opposite direction away from the herd. My wrangler yelled, "Go git 'im Annie". So I pulled up my stampede strap, turned my hos' around and chased the calf. I think I was in Wyoming before I caught it. Eventually I returned this wayward critter back into the herd, next to the bull where it had come from.

Without warning, the big, red eyed bull with 2 metres of horns, put his head down, bellowed and charged me for all he was worth. In a very weak voice I screamed at my wrangler, "This one's yours, I am getting the hell out of here".

It had been very hot all day, reaching 100° and it surprised me that after drinking something like 3 litres of water, I didn't need to relieve myself once. I think I sweated it out through my pores or somewhere. It could have been the fact that I was not prepared to squat in rattler country. This in my opinion is where men have a distinct advantage over women.

Finally, we were back at the camp site which had been demolished while we were away. It looked as if it had been hit by a storm. The cowpokes loaded all the gear into various dilapidated trucks and us into an estate truck. As there was not enough room for us all, some of the people were loaded into the open back of the truck. They were subjected to the tremendous dust cloud we were kicking up, as well as crickets, wind and heat. Driving at speed, we were unable to see the road in front of us due to another of our trucks being ahead and kicking up dust. We drove through the mountains to Battle Creek to spend the next few nights in this location. It was beautiful.

On the cattle drive the next day I saw my first wild life, a deer in the mountains. The camp site was at the foot of the mountains, complete with a fresh water 'Crik' and trout. I thought a 'crik' was what you had in your neck, but it's a fresh mountain creek.

The camp was made and we were assigned our sleeping quarters, foams and sleeping bags. Then, without warning, a dust storm blew up and swept through the camp like a tornado, taking all the tents with it. We managed to rescue most of them, and dumped them into a very ancient barn, with a crooked door.

After chow, we were entertained by a group of young American violinists. The youngest one was eight and the oldest was 65. They stood in the open prairie and played Country and Western music and songs from the shows.

The shooting stars were out and the wranglers told me they had formed a queue and were ready for me whenever I felt like a few more tears.

We were then given a fabulous display of horsemanship, and were told that this is how you should do it.

Then came bed time. The barn was the only place to sleep in. 50 men and women shared the barn that night. Cowboys still chew tobacco, and they snore all night. We ladies got little or no sleep.

My horse was now changed as I now knew why he was called Houdini. I was given Cherokee. He was very different from Houdini, most of the time he was where I left him. His main problem was that he didn't mind drinking water, but crossing it was another matter entirely.

During that day on a long drive we crossed many creeks. By the end of the day Cherokee decided he had got his feet wet too often. All the cattle had crossed this last wide creek, but when it was my turn the horse refused to go and stopped abruptly at the edge of the creek.

I twice tried to get him over to no avail. He went round in circles, reared on his hind legs, bucked and did everything in his power to unseat me. He was not successful. The wranglers had by now given me a nickname. I am known throughout Montana as Bostik Bum.

I asked Monty, my wrangler, how to get across. He said, "Yes Ann, there is a way". I suddenly didn't like the tone of his voice. "How do I do it? I asked. He said, "Up with your stampede, strap turn your horse around, go back about 200 yards and get into a nice steady lope". This is cowboy for canter. "Then what happens?" He told me that when you get near to the creek there is a good chance that your horse will continue to go. I said, "What do I do if he won't go?" I was told that they would all dry me out on the way back. It gives one a lovely warm feeling to know that you have friends who will always help you in your hour of need.

So, without further ado, I tightened my stampede strap under my chin, turned my horse round 200 yards and began to approach the creek at a very steady canter, whilst screaming in terror. On arrival at the creek, what did the horse do? He took off and jumped over the creek. I have never jumped on a horse before. Taking off is easy, it's the coming down that is a BIT painful.

You probably know that western saddles are slightly different to English ones. They are bigger, softer and have leather stirrups instead of hard metal ones. They also have a large pommel at the front. This is a great piece of equipment on which to hang your lasso, your make up, your handbag and your hairdryer. I came down on the pommel on the bone at the front of my body, and parts of me went a very delicate shade of black. It taught me some very valuable lessons. Whenever on a difficult manoeuvre, always hold the pommel so that you know where it is. It is also the reason why all cowboys yell out Yi! Ha! Usually in a high pitched voice.

Once across the river I did a lot of cantering and trotting, American style, I hasten to add. I was now covered in dust from top to toe and filthy. There is no one to see me except cowboys and cows though. The facilities were still very basic and primitive.

After chow that evening I was taught by a wrangler how to lasso a cow. I hasten to add that I am now competent at this task, providing the cow is standing still and I am not galloping on a horse. The same wrangler, who performs in rodeos, taught me how to crack a bull whip. This is not as easy as it looks. It requires great upper arm and shoulder strength. After beating myself across the back on more than one occasion I finally mastered this art. I can now move a Coca Cola can around a field with a bull whip. But seriously, who would want to move a Coca Cola can around a field with a bull whip. If, upon reading this fascinating piece of information you would like me to teach you this piece of real cowboy artwork, you bring the coke and I'll bring the whip.

Bed that night was very welcome, and to be able to investigate the bruising and apply some lotion.

The next morning came round all too soon and I was awoken with yet another tick call at 5.15am on this morning. Breakfast was corn bread and scrambled eggs and at 7 am we saddled up.

Today we planned to bring in over 200 head of cattle, through the most beautiful, lonesome prairie I have ever seen. We even had a stampede caused by the dogs helping with the round up. We asked the wranglers where they would like us to go. Their language being very colourful doesn't permit me to say more. Suffice to say, roughly translated, they asked us to go up the mountain at full canter and get out of the way. I can assure you we needed no second asking.

Once the stampede was almost under control they very politely asked us if we would, now come down from the mountain and help with the final calming down.

The temperature was 98°. Dealing with 200 head of stampeding cattle in that degree of heat was an experience that will take me a long time to forget. The way the wranglers dealt with this was like watching a true western adventure.

We rode through 'Criks', where many of the horses fought to get at the water, which eventually caused a fight for possession. Two riders and their horses at this point, took an early bath. Well, at least they were cleaner than I was.

After 5 hours in the saddle the chuck wagons caught us up again and served lunch, followed by another ride of two hours back to Battle Creek and camp.

All the 'girls' from our tent decided we could not live with the dirt any longer. So, wearing just shorts and a bra, carrying a towel and shampoo we trundled to the crik. Fresh mountain water is very cold. We had been in the saddle for over six hours in high temperatures and I can assure you that your body temperature is a bit warm. Getting into the icy cold water commanded a feat of courage and stupidity.

Finally we were all sitting down in at least 18 inches of water and putting shampoo all over our bodies. There were fresh mountain trout swimming by on either side of me. They were the cleanest trout that Montana had ever seen.

After a well deserved and much refreshed rest, a supper of beef ribs and the traditional baked beans were served.

If only I had known what was coming next I would have not bathed in the creek. A big yellow school bus arrived to take us for the 4 hour ride down the mountain to a one hos' town to have a Jacuzzi.

None of us bought bathing costumes, but we were told, don't worry, as you walk into the bath house you will be given a towel, looked up and down and sized for a hire costume. The only size they had left for me was a costume that had belonged to a very pregnant lady. On entering the water, the pocket of the costume filled. The cowboys commented that they knew things happened quickly in America but this was a record.

The spa was hot sulphur water coming straight off the mountains. Sulphur water is very good for aching bones. The temperature was 100°. Getting in had taken quite a long time, as the body needs to adjust. Once in and seated this was luxury beyond compare.

One of the wranglers was soaking next to me and he said, "Annie, do you know Amazing Grace?" He told me that this song is the 'national anthem' of their ranch. At the end of a perfect round up, everyone sits on a bale of hay round the camp fire, watching the shooting stars, eating baked beans, and singing this anthem. I said, "Please don't say any more, I could burst into tears any moment now." He said, "I know you can sing so please start now". Which I did, and he harmonised with me. He had a beautiful voice and within minutes there were nearly 30 people in the jacuzzi all joining in with the singing. As you can imagine, it was a very big jacuzzi. This was America. We then became known as the 'Cattle Drive Choristers'. We sat in the spa for at least two and a half hours singing everything that reminded us of cowboys and westerns. Eventually I had to get out as I looked just like a prune.

Outside there was a very warm swimming pool, much cooler than the jacuzzi, but still sulphur water. We played water polo and lots of silly water games, until a thunder storm with large hailstones descended upon us. My arms were getting bruised, so I decided it was time to leave the pool.

After a refreshing shower, the school bus returned, driving us back into the mountains, a very cold tent and an even colder sleeping bag.

The next morning we were spoilt as we had a lay in until 5.30am. After breakfast and a visit to the portaloo, the horses were saddled, and loaded onto trailers. We humans were also loaded into trailers, and drove for one hour along a horrendous narrow mountain road. I think they call these tracks roads.

The cowboy I was with at the front of the truck, drove all the time with only one hand on the steering wheel, the other hand was smoking a cigarette. To unnerve me even more he told dirty jokes and laughed the whole time. Of course, I also laughed; I didn't want to upset him.

On arrival at the designated spot, we crawled out of the trucks filthy dirty, mounted our horses and rode off into the mountains looking for strays. The vastness of this area in unbelievable. We saw no one else all morning, not even a stray Indian. I heard some cows mooing in the distance, so the wranglers and some cowpokes set off to see if they could be located.

At this point I and three other rookies were told to stay where we were at 8,500 ft and wait to be collected. Nobody came back for us. After two hours alone we began to realise that we had been forgotten. We dismounted and tied the horses under some trees as it was very hot.

Standing on the very edge of the mountain, we called for help, we whistled, we called for Geronimo and finally we all sang one verse of "Amazing Grace". Nobody came. We were now running very low on water and getting a little bit disturbed.

After collectively discussing our problem we decided that we would try to find the trail back down the mountain. On the way up I had noticed some pylons on my right hand side. I suggested that if we kept them on our left hand side going down we might find civilisation.

After a very hairy ride of some two hours we finally found the trailers, one dog, but no humans. We decided to wait for a while. After about 20 minutes we were joined by some more lost cowpokes. Being very smart, we joined forces and tried to find the chuck wagon. We had eaten nothing since 5.30am and it was now 2.30pm.

We rode over hills and draws but still could not find what we needed. Later that afternoon we came across some other ranchers who said they had seen our chuck wagon and would send it down to us. Very much relieved by this news we dismounted and tied our horses in the shade and waited for rescue.

The temperature was only 93°, we had been in the saddle for over six hours. We had run out of water, had nothing to eat, but we were all cowboys now and we knew we had to cope.

After what seemed like an eternity the chuck wagon arrived amidst cheers from us all. Unfortunately the cook had forgotten to pack the bread, so we had a sandwich without bread and I can assure you that's not easy. The water was more important. I didn't know I could drink one litre without stopping for breath.

The trailer finally arrived and took us back to camp. What a day we had all had. We found no strays; we were abandoned at 8,500 ft with no water, no food, and no wranglers to help us. This was real cowboy stuff. I liked it.

Back at the camp site, we told the ranch owners of our bit of excitement during the day. Each wrangler thought the other one was looking after us. Then it dawned on us, we had not even been missed. This made us feel very special.

After chow, I had a small wash, put on a clean shirt and a pair of trainers. This evening we were being entertained by a live country and western band playing dance music for us in the old barn. Bubba, one of the wranglers, asked me if I could Rock 'n' Roll. I told him that in my younger days I used to give demonstrations of this art. I said that as I was now 64, had been up to ten hours every day in the saddle for the past six days, have severe arthritic knees, I don't think I can still cut a rug". Before I could object he carried me onto the barn dance boards and we started to Rock 'n' Roll.

Everyone started to clap and cheer, as for a while I could still do it. Unfortunately, I couldn't breathe, but that seemed to bother no one. Each wrangler in turn danced with me. Eventually both knees caved in and I fell on to the dance floor amongst the straw. I was ceremoniously lifted and placed on a bale of hay where I had to watch everyone else have fun for the rest of the evening.

By 1am we all fell into bed ready for sleep, which did not come. That night the temperature went down to 32°. I shivered and my body suffered cramp all night long. But I survived, JUST.

By 7.00am the next morning we received our famous Tick Call. There were two reasons I was glad to hear him. One to get up and get warm and two to realise we had been given a lay in. Breakfast was not until 8.00am. Sitting around the camp fire, at last feeling warm and eating hot pancakes was luxury.

After food came the statutory visit to the usual offices, watering the horses and loading the saddle bags ready for the day. Today, there seemed to be some slight disagreement between the wranglers as to which area needed to be checked for strays. It wasn't until 9.45am that we finally rode out of the camp. To me, the day had nearly gone. I had normally been in the saddle for three hours by this time.

Our task today, was to round up strays in another mountainous area. I have never ridden a horse before at such an acute angle. The mountain slopes consisted of loose slates and gofer holes.

On reaching the top of the mountain we stopped to answer a call of nature, drink and apply more chap stick to very sore dry lips and sun block to the parts of the body that were showing. We then spotted a herd of cows, bulls and calves in a very deep draw. I hope every one appreciates my knowledge of cowboy vocabulary!

The wranglers divided all the cowboys into three groups. Group number one to head up the cows. Group number two to head them off. Group number three to check all the draws for any more strays. I acquired the short straw and was assigned to group number three. A draw is a deep gulley between two high rising sides of the mountain. Climbing down on horseback is interesting, to say the least. I had to lean heavily backwards, just like John Wayne did in his movies, pick your route very carefully so as not to get stuck at the bottom of the draw. Once I had arrived safely at the bottom, I then had to kick the horse, who then jumps over the last little bit of water and then canters at speed up the steep climb. It is important here to lean forward, hanging on to the pommel for dear life. The pommel is a very important part of the saddle. It does two things; one: - it stops you falling off, if you hold onto it and two: - it stops it digging into your private parts.

On reaching the top of the draw, this process is repeated time after time, after time. After over three more hours in the saddle performing this task, I saw two deer, but not one cow. I personally felt very confident in reporting to my wrangler that there 'ain't no cows or strays in my draws'.

In my group there were five riders, so my wrangler with two others told us that they would go left and send myself and one other straight ahead just to check the last and final draws. We were suddenly completely alone in the Montana Mountains with no one else in sight. Very frightening.

At long last, we met up and rode to within sight of our camp. A great debate took place as we were on top of the mountain and the cows were at the bottom, and so was our camp. My wrangler decided to head back the way we had come. From our vantage point I was able to watch the cowpokes drive the cattle through a very narrow gulley and wash.

Eventually we all met up and herded the cows, calves and bulls across the plain, through many more criks. My next task was to get the cattle and my horse to jump down the deep sides of the creek, paddle for a while and then jump out the other side. In some very small way it was similar to the behaviour of migratory bison.

I noticed a few strays hiding in the brush so I decided to be a true wrangler and chase them out to rejoin the herd. Once the herd were happily settled in the pasture we rode back to camp for a well earned rest and drink, some goodies to eat, a snooze, relay some jokes and share life' experiences.

At around 5.00pm we had to mount up again. The plan now was to bring some 150 head of cattle into the corral, to enable the wranglers to separate the bulls from the cows and calves. The ranch had enough calves for the season and did not wish to have any more.

Herding them into the corral was not easy. The temperature was 100° and the dry dust was choking, making breathing difficult. The only way to breathe was by soaking my bandana with cold water and putting it over my nose. I now felt just like Jesse James about to rob a train.

To hear 150 head of cattle moo and complain, 30 cowpokes yelling 'Yi! Ha!', 'Move 'em out', 'Head 'em up' has to be experienced to comprehend the fantastic work done by all.

As soon as the cattle were all enclosed and the gate shut, the next task was to separate the bulls from the cows. As you can imagine the bulls did not take kindly to this task.

As a beginner I could not take part in this, it was too dangerous. My job was to help keep the cows and the calves away from the bulls. The bulls were put into one gated corral whilst the beginners put the cows and calves in another. This process took over two hours in the heat of the day. I was now so dirty and dusty, even my best friends wouldn't have recognised me.

On completion, another gate was opened and the mums and babies were let into the pasture. As I was helping drive the cattle through, I said to a wrangler. "Excuse me, but there is one cow here with a piece of equipment that doesn't match all the others." One of the bulls had escaped detection and he had nearly 60 cows all to himself. I said, "I expect he thinks it's his birthday". "That will probably keep me busy until supper time, what shall I do this evening?" may have passed through the bull's mind. The language became a bit colourful again at this time. Galloping ahead we managed to turn the lead cow around. Providing she turns, all the rest will follow. We got all the cows, calves and the one errant bull back into the corral. The wranglers did me the honour of allowing me to help put this critter into the corral with the rest of his mates.

The next job was to herd the mums and babies a mile away to their pasture, then another mile ride to get back to camp. On this day I had been six hours in the saddle working very hard. Who said this was a holiday? I began to realise that I had paid money for this privilege. Daft woman.

On arrival back at the camp I first took my horse to water and then I took myself to water. I now felt so dry, dirty and dusty that I decided to have a strip wash in my tent.

Soon steak, black eyed peas, corn on the cob, jacket potato and the obligatory baked beans were served. I was very hungry.

Then, this being our last night, the fun began. We were all sitting in a circle around the camp fire, seated on bales of hay, and given a certificate of competence to prove that we were successful and experienced wranglers.

After toasting marshmallows and relaying adventures of the week, a wrangler produced his guitar and said to me, "We know you can play, give us a song or two". My tears began to well up at this moment. When I had finished my singing, I handed the guitar back to the wrangler. It was now time to sing our anthem. All standing together around the camp fire with our arms around each other, the guitar gently strumming, the shooting stars overhead doing what shooting stars do, we at last started to sing Amazing Grace.

For the first time that week I was not the only person who shed a few tears of emotion. To live with the wranglers in Montana, round up cattle, work in close proximity with people you don't know and not wash for a week, I can assure you all is very tear jerking.

More marshmallows were toasted, chaps were branded, we told jokes and stories, played the guitar and sang under the stars until very early the next morning.

Nobody wanted this night to end. Everyone's wit and sense of humour was tremendous.

After breakfast the next day we all said our very tearful farewells. Eventually, I had to leave for Bozeman airport, ready for the long journey home and back to normality.

One of my lifetimes' ambition had at last been fulfilled. I've laughed, cried and enjoyed every moment and can't wait to do it again.

At times the going was rough, basic, hot, dusty and tiring, but, even though my family and friends said, "You must be mad to attempt this at your age, you'll be sorry." I can now report that I was never stiff, never sore, no headaches and I never regretted one tiny moment. I can happily report that, SADDLE SORE IN MONTANA IS NOT TRUE.

I got a good seat on the airplane home. People kept sniffing and giving me a funny look. I can't think why.

The following year I went to Wyoming, where I learnt to rope and throw, brand cattle and how to give medication to calves that have the scours. That's diarrhoea to you and me.

The year after I went back to Montana to the same ranch as before. Of course I was now a bit more experienced. This time it was castration time. I only watched this. What is removed is a delicacy and they are called prairie oysters. I recommend you read the menu very carefully from now on. After Montana I went to Oklahoma for my fourth round up. This is where the "Wind comes sweeping down the planes". It appeared as if the ranch owner owned half of Oklahoma. I could ride all day, see nobody but still be on his land. WOW!

I will admit I am getting older, but submit, not yet.

Me - Driving chuck wagon

My first introduction to 'Houdini'

"I'm going to catch me some cattle with my new lasso"

Rounding up cattle in the rolling hills of Wyoming.

101

Branding and castration time

A typical working loo - This is the luxury version with the built in horse rail.

"Dusty" - At the end of a days roundup.

THE MAFIA AND I CONQUERED MOUNT ETNA.

My adventure started at least one year before the actual event. So I thought I'd give you a little background.

As I have already said my husband and I owned seven Hardware retail outlets in Surrey, an Interflora Florist, a Lawnmower engineering workshop, plus our own wholesale company which was started in the loft of our bungalow.

All good quality Ironmongers belonged to an association called The

London and Southern Counties Ironmongers Association. As we obviously met these criteria we belonged to the above association which had 5,000 members. Mainly men.

Every year the committee organised a week long conference, sometimes in England but mostly in foreign parts. This would consist of a day and a half of business plus five and a half days of whooping it up with your fellow traders. This was known as a business expense as far as the accountant was concerned.

On one particular occasion we attempted to book a conference in Sicily. Unfortunately, I think it had something to do with the fact that we did not cross the palm of the Godfather with enough of the 'readies'. All the hotels seemed to be booked, there were no aeroplanes flying during the week we wanted and no coaches available for tours around the island.

The committee in their wisdom booked us into the Isle of Wight instead. Something that was highly enjoyable was sitting around the swimming pool with your mates, sipping cocktails, basking in the sun and discussing the price of creosote.

A few years later, I was given the dubious honour of being the first and only ever Lady President of the London and Southern Counties Ironmongers Association. At the same time, I was also voted the first ever Lady on to the Board of Management of the British Hardware Federation. Not a lot of people have ever heard of these two organisations, so you can see what an important individual I am.

In this exhalted capacity, I was given the opportunity to decide where to hold my conference. I had never been to Sicily before and I had never seen a live volcano, so this had to be my choice.

Through the travel agents, we tried to get this in motion. To make sure this would be possible, I suggested to my secretary that both he and I and the tour operator should go to Sicily for a weekend. The object being to not only meet the Godfather but also to ascertain that the hotels and the coaches would be available at our disposal. I also suggested that the tour operator, who was part Sicilian and spoke the language, should let it be known to the Mafia that his island wished to be visited by the London and Southern Counties Ironmongers Association. I also felt it was imperative, that if possible, we should cross the Godfather's palm with silver as often as possible during the weekend.

On arrival at the airport who should meet us but the Godfather himself to welcome this important V.I.P. from England. He kissed the back of my hand, which I hasten to add I have since washed, and welcomed me to his island. He said, "Follow me I have a Mafia staff car waiting outside". I thanked him profusely and immediately crossed his palm with silver. It's surprising how money talks. I felt at this moment how important it was to be on the right side and not the left side of the Godfather.

In the staff car we were taken to a fabulous five star hotel with all the conference facilities needed. After being treated to lunch we boarded the staff car again and were given a private tour of the island taking in sights, vineyards and many places of interest. Every time we stopped I crossed his palm once more. By the end of the day we were quite good friends, I think he fancied the President of the London and Southern Counties Ironmongers Association.

Suddenly, any hotel we liked the look of was ours for the asking, which ever date we wanted to fly was available to us and whichever tour we decided upon, all we had to do (according to the Godfather) was whistle.

On arrival back in England we started taking bookings for the Sicily conference. It proved to be very popular and upon reaching two hundred we decided to close the bookings as the aeroplane and the hotel could only take that amount.

At one of the Board of Management meetings, the committee asked me if I would write and produce a show to close the conference. Being the idiot that I am, I said yes. I started searching for suitable thespians amongst my colleagues and holding auditions in England. If any of you readers have ever taken part in amateur dramatics you will know that more fun is had at rehearsals than on the night.

Finally the show was put together. You probably are aware that to work with plumbers in this capacity, writing many sketches, the language can be colourful as many of the items are named after parts of the body. I will leave you to use your own imagination.

Many props and costumes were needed to bring from England as I was unaware what I would be able to buy in Sicily let alone find the time for such exploits.

Getting through customs at Gatwick with not only excess baggage but a small attaché case containing the very large chain of office as worn by the President, presented no problems at all. Once I had explained that I was President of the London and Southern Counties Ironmongers Association, everything else seemed to be easy.

My first problem arose in Sicily airport. I was trying to explain why I was carrying two chambers, one broom, one bucket, one guitar, four fairy wings, four fairy wands and twenty old time hats. The customs guard thought I was either a drug smuggler or had escaped from the local asylum. As I do not speak the language making myself understood was impossible. Without warning, with an armed guard either side of me, I was dragged into a nearby shed. It was at this juncture, I thought I would never see England again. In a little panic I suggested that the guards find my secretary Tom, in the arrivals lounge, who would vouch for my authenticity. As my secretary, like me, was unable to converse in Sicilian I was still no further forward. At this point I asked Tom, if he would return to the lounge to see if the tour operator had arrived. Within minutes she returned with the Godfather who had also arrived to welcome the Ironmongers to his island. He said, "Where is the President?" she replied that she had been arrested and was in the customs shed with two armed guards.

On entering the shed, he immediately spoke to the guards in their own tongue. You don't need to be able to speak the language to pick up the tone of voice. He then turned to me and asked me why I was carrying two chambers; we do have facilities in Sicily. I told him that we were putting on a show at the end of the conference and these are some of the props needed, He asked me, "What on earth are you going to do with two chambers?" I told him that two male ironmongers will be dressed in nighties and sitting on the chambers singing a song. At this point his face was a picture. I said, "Trust me that's what they are going to do". He then asked me which song they were going to sing. I told him it was called, "When I was a wee wee tot". He decided that the only way I could convince the guards that I was not mad, was to perform this act.

Other people come on holiday to relax and have fun but not me. How many other holiday makers have to sing to not only the Godfather but the customs guards as well, before being allowed into the country?

I sat on a chamber placed on a chair and started to sing the song which has three verses. At the end of each verse I was made to wait whilst the Godfather translated the meaning into language the guards could understand. I think this totally convinced them all that I really was mad.

When the song was finished the Godfather asked me "What happens next?" Polystyrene worms found in packing cases, are put into the chambers and thrown at the audience at the end of the song. Obviously, this is not what the audience expects. One or two of the guards even smiled at this point, I thought I was winning.

However, the next question was, "What are you going to do with the wings and the wands?" I became agitated at this point. What more must I do to escape their clutches? I knew now I had to perform the next act called, 'Nobody loves a fairy when she's forty' which, on the night would be performed by male Ironmongers wearing long johns and tutu's. The wands being made from plumbers bending springs enabled the ends to wobble. I told the guards you will only get one verse for free. The last line of the first verse being, "Your Fairy days are ending, when your wand has started bending, nobody loves a fairy when she's old". Having now performed this one verse, I am sure that the guards and the Godfather decided that they couldn't win.

The Godfather told me that all charges against me had been waived. He relieved me of two chambers and one broom and in a very efficient voice said, "Follow me".

Four large coaches were waiting outside to take us to our five star hotel. We settled in, unpacked and made the final plans for the start of the conference.

The next day and a half of business sessions, were not only very successful but very well attended.

We now had five and a half days to enjoy the amenities of the island. One of the very popular trips was to visit Mount Etna. At least forty five people had booked this trip on a day that was not available to me as I was still finalising the conference. I suggested this party go ahead without me as there was another ten people who wished to go the following day. As I had never visited an active volcano before I requested that everyone on the first trip described to me in full detail the events of the day on their return.

By 9.00.a.m. the next morning the party was ready to board the coach. Each person was supplied with a snack lunch and a can of drink. The temperature was a very warm 80 degrees. I cheerfully waved them off on their tour, asking them to keep a careful note of the exploits of the day.

By 7.00 p.m. I was waiting outside the Hotel to greet their return. As the coach pulled up outside I rushed to greet them. I couldn't wait to hear about their day on Mount Etna.

Once inside and refreshed, we all sat around the pool while I started asking many questions. Their replies put a bit of a damper on my expectations.

"We had a very boring four and a half hour coach ride to the other side of the island to the foot hills of Mount Etna in the village of Bronte. We were told to get off the coach and start to walk up the mountain dirt path holding onto a rope. We had only gone about half way when we were told that Mount Etna was rumbling. We turned around, held the rope in the other hand and descended. We boarded the coach, had another boring four and a half hour ride and here we are." I was stunned. I felt that I couldn't wait for my turn the next day.

Never daunted, the next day dawned bright warm and very sunny. I felt ready for my adventure and was feeling optimistic. There were now a total of twenty Ironmongers ready for this trip. The hotel gave us the obligatory packed lunch and a can of drink.

Just before boarding the coach, a Mafia staff car arrived, containing the Godfather. He said to me, "It's been a long time since I visited Mount Etna, can I spend the day with you?" I replied, "Of course you can, we will be very honoured." I couldn't possibly say no to such an influential person.

By 10.00.a.m we were ready. The temperature had now risen to a mere 85° so all of us dressed accordingly. My outfit consisted of, a pair of shorts, a T shirt, a pair of flip flops and a 'cardie', just in case.

We suffered the very boring four and a half hour coach ride to the village of Bronte which is at the foot hills of Mount Etna. On leaving the air conditioned coach we were visibly shaken as the temperature had climbed to 95°. I felt as if not only the volcano would erupt but given half the chance I could as well.

We then, courtesy of the Godfather boarded an eight soft wheeled "Moon buggy", which then proceeded to drive up the 1972 lava flow. This proved to be quite exciting as every so often the lava flow moved and therefore so did the buggy. I can only compare this ride to what it must be like on the moon. It was a vast empty space with nothing green in sight, no wild life visible and no singing birds. It was imperative to hold onto a grab rail in front of your seat, otherwise all that would be visible was someone else's feet.

Two youngsters, off spring of our party, were crying in terror. Nothing seemed to able to calm them down. Not even stern looks from 'You know who'. It was suggested they go to the front of the buggy and sit on

"Auntie Ann's lap." That's me. I now have two very frightened children, one on each knee. To drive away the gremlins I started to sing, 'Whenever I feel afraid, I hold my head erect'. The sound of my voice was enough to make them instantly stop crying.

Eventually we arrived at a very level plateau and were told to get off here as the incline was now too steep for the buggy to go any further.

Something happens to your body when you are being bounced around, the temperature is getting colder and you are a bit nervous. We were ushered into a mountain café and offered hot mulled cider. We all declined the offer until we had found the toilets. There were no Ladies and Gents, just toilets, but as we were all friends we piled in together. The Ladies amongst us were poised ready to get in first. Two reasons for this, Ladies first would be polite, and we take longer than the men.

Standing next to me in line was a young Sicilian, obviously not in our party, perhaps staff from the café. Frequently he nudged my elbow and muttered something in his native tongue. I said, "I don't speak your language I am British, please be quiet". This didn't work and he nudged me again. This time I said, "Don't speak to me in that tone of voice I am a V.I.P from England and the President of the London and Southern Counties Ironmongers Association". You can imagine this too had no effect. He eventually nudged me again and said, "You look". I turned to him and very loudly said, "WHAT?"

He had undone his trousers and was flashing me in the toilets half way up Mount Etna. I have to be honest I laughed at him because the weather was getting colder and I think he was wasting his time. I nudged the male Ironmonger next to me in the queue and said, "You look". He said, "Don't you start". He eventually looked and also laughed. Then we passed this message along the line until the toilet rang to the sound of happy laughter. Two of my friends grabbed him by the arms and took him outside to deliver him to the Godfather. We never saw him again. Having at long last satisfied the need we trooped back outside to see what would happen next.

The Godfather was having a very heated exchange with what looked like a mountain guide. Being the person 'in charge' I asked what the problem was. He told me that as the weather was deteriorating the guide thought it would be dangerous to take a party of British Ironmongers to the top of the mountain. I knew that the guide knew much more than I did and was prepared to abide by his decision.

The Godfather said, roughly translated, "I have told him that if he values his life, his wife and his knee caps he will take his party as far as they wish to go and bring them all back alive".

The temperature was now considerably colder in fact it was only about 45°, the cloud base was lowering, there was a flurry of snow in the air and the wind was beginning to blow. It would be impossible to go any further dressed as we all were in shorts, T shirt, flip flops and a 'cardie.'

The next stop was a mountain hut where we were each supplied with either an Army greatcoat or an R.A.F. greatcoat. My R.A.F. coat had obviously belonged to a man who was at least 6 foot, 6 inches tall. Not only was it very wet from a previous visit but it hung on the ground at least 12 inches below my feet. It was impossible to find my hands. Undaunted I wrapped the coat around my body and tied the belt.

On putting my hands in the pockets, I found a polythene bag, which I tied onto my head to keep the wind out of my ears. If any of you have ever worn a polythene bag on your head you will know that it is impossible to hear what anyone is saying to you.

The guide then looked at our feet. Flip flops are not suitable wear to climb Mount Etna. We were ushered into yet another mountain hut and supplied with rubber over boots. The only size they had left for me was size eleven. I do take a size eight, but I can assure you they were *a bit too big*. Nevertheless if that is all that is available, I will have to make do. I then delicately slipped my size eight into the size eleven.

On stepping out onto the level plateau again dressed in large coat, polythene bag on my head, size eleven over boots, I was met by the Godfather. I looked at him and said, "I'm yours; take me when you're ready". Fortunately all he did was laugh.

We then duly presented ourselves to our very brave guide, to receive final instructions.

Our numbers were now down to ten due to the fact that the children were too young to take part in this adventure plus another eight adults who felt that they were not tired of living yet and decided to remain by the log fire drinking cider. How sensible!

The guide then said that if there were any people who had high blood pressure or a dodgy ticker, now was the time to own up. Mount Etna, give or take an eruption or two is at present 11,000 feet above sea level. At that height, due to the cold, the sulphur and less pressure, this could make breathing very difficult.

The less pressure the harder it is for your body to absorb oxygen.

At this stage four more folks decided that this trip was not for them.

The final instructions were as follows. We must always hold the belt of the person in front and never, under any circumstances let go. Do not stray from the footprints left in the snow by the person in front of you. Let the guide know the instant you are unhappy with the conditions. I knew this would be an adventure, I could feel the hair rising at the nape of my neck.

We were now six in total, four men and two women.

With trepidation we started the climb. To pretend we were not frightened we even sang, 'Hi Ho, Hi Ho it's off to work we go'.

The higher we climbed the colder it became. It was now blowing a gale force wind, a severe blizzard, the cloud base almost level with our chests and the temperature was minus 10 degrees. The snow was now shin deep and filling my large boots. The terrain became more difficult, and oxygen was getting scarce. The sulphur, blowing in our direction, hurt not only your throat but you could begin to feel it burn the lungs.

However, we were not down hearted. True British grit takes over here. Many stops were needed to try to warm our hands over the many blow holes. As you can imagine with temperatures at this level, it plays havoc with the bladder. There was no way I was prepared to squat over a blow hole. I did feel that even if I had an accident in that department, it would freeze as it left me.

After what seemed like many hours the line of people came to an abrupt halt. One of the ladies in the group was having difficulty in breathing and it was quite obvious she needed help. The guide asked us to stay together in a tight bunch, and not move. We had to wait here while he took the lady down to 2,000 feet where she could breathe, and we had to wait for him to come back for us all. He had had an argument with the Godfather, and he could've said that we were lost in the clouds, never to be seen again. To be left alone on Mount Etna in temperatures of minus 10 degrees, a severe gale, a blizzard, knee deep in snow, trying to breathe whilst inhaling sulphur worried us just a little. Supposing he never came back.

Fortunately he returned some 20 minutes later. It had been the longest twenty minutes of my life.

With now only five in our party we started to ascend once more. Singing was no longer possible. Trying to breathe was all we were concerned with.

The visibility was now at zero, it was minus 12 degrees, and my hands and feet seemed to belong to someone else, because I couldn't feel them at all. My finger tips were very painful and I was experiencing pins and needles. As it was impossible to see the person in front, I would, from time to time, give a hearty yank on the belt to make sure there was some resistance. I think the person behind me had the same feelings as occasionally I was pulled backwards.

It had now reached the stage where the only way to make headway was to lean very far forward, otherwise if you stood upright, the wind would blow you over backwards. Every time one foot was put down you had to take a very deep breath. By the time the next foot went down there was no more breath in the lungs. I was not sure that I would survive this escapade.

Our guide who was obviously young and virile was *running* up and down the line asking us if we wanted to continue. We did not have enough breath to climb and talk at the same time. We asked him to run his hand along our arm until it reached the hand. If our thumb was in the upright position we would continue. If it was in the downward position we would abort.

Some very strange things freeze under these conditions. As the water dripped off the end of my nose it froze and formed a small icicle. It did save me having to find a hanky, I could just snap off the offending icicle. One gentleman in our group had a moustache which grew some quite dramatic icicles. The hair in his nostrils and ears also froze. I was luckier than the men, only my eyebrows and eyelashes froze. Each time I blinked it became painful.

Suddenly the person in front of me came to an abrupt halt, causing us all to bump into each other.

The guide told us that it would be too dangerous for him to take all of us at once, to the crater rim. He would be prepared to take us one at a time.

Only two of us were stupid enough to say, "Yes please".

I would at this point like to paint the picture.

We were five English Ironmongers dressed in the strangest outfits, it was freezing cold; we were at 11,000 feet-ish up a very active volcano. The visibility was at zero, the temperature was now minus 15°, and some very young Sicilian guide asks me if I would like to go to the crater rim with him alone. If only I could breathe I would have screamed with excitement.

Four of us remained huddled together alone while the guide took one gentleman in our party, we hoped, just to the edge of the crater rim. It seemed like another eternity that we felt abandoned. Supposing this time he really didn't come back for us. Suddenly from out of the clouds the two of them appeared.

Before I could say, "Is it my turn now?" The guide grabbed me by the hand and *ran* with me to the crater rim. There was no way I was going to let go of his hand. Wherever I went he was going with me. He stopped very suddenly and pointed and said, "You look". I thought for a moment it could be the flasher, but I was wrong.

I was now standing on top of the crater rim of Mount Etna, looking across the caldera. I could see everything, it was as clear as a bell. If it was snowing there, it would be melting long before it got anywhere near the crater. The difference in visibility was fantastic. Looking one way, I could see forever, looking another way, I could see nothing. Even the snow in my boots was beginning to melt, and I began to feel warm for the first time since starting the climb.

I asked the guide, how do you know when she's going to blow? He replied, "Trust me, a split second after it blows you know all about it". He also told me that it had been rumbling for quite a few days. I suggested that we get the hell out of here as soon as possible. Seeing this sight is something that will live with me forever.

All too soon he turned me round and we finally made it back to the four we left behind.

As we walked down the mountain, the lower we descended the warmer it became. To be able at last to feel my extremities was a relief. On arrival back at the mountain hut, the first place most visited was the toilets. We looked every where for the flasher, but he was long gone. The clothing was returned to the mountain huts, and the thoughts of the big log fire and a large glass of hot mulled cider made us feel warmer just thinking about it.

The Godfather who had not joined us on this last leg of our journey was still in the mountain hut and expressed his delight at seeing all of us return safely and in one piece.

After warming in front of the fire and drinking the cider we began to feel warmer, but it was still possible to feel how cold the internal body organs were.

We boarded the moon buggy and made the perilous journey to the bottom of the mountain. The temperature here was 95 degrees. It was almost impossible to comprehend. On boarding the coach, still shivering we asked the driver if he would put the heater on for a while. Reluctantly he agreed, but very soon there was so much condensation inside that this was very quickly turned off.

By the time we had travelled for four and a half hours back to the hotel we felt a little warmer. As we pulled into the forecourt, it seemed that everyone at the hotel rushed out to see if we were O.K. We hadn't noticed the time. It was nearly 8.00.p.m. and we had been gone for over ten hours. The news had reported that the volcano was rumbling and could blow at any moment. I don't think that the Mafia was worried about the President of the London and Southern Counties Ironmongers Association, but probably the fact that the Godfather had been with us for the day.

There were helicopters on search and rescue and all the Mafia staff cars were touring the island looking for us.

It was a relief to get into the hotel, where a hot meal followed by a long soak in a hot bath was waiting. The group who had gone the day before couldn't wait to hear of our exciting exploits. "You will have to wait till the morning", we said, "All we need at the moment is a long rest".

After breakfast the next morning, we sat around the pool, surrounded by interested Ironmongers re-living our exploits of the day before. I think most of them were jealous as we had much more excitement than they did.

The following evening was time to put on our show in the hotel. We invited the Godfather to be our guest, plus as many of the hotel staff that would like to attend. It was strange to watch the Sicilians trying to understand English humour. From time to time they laughed but mostly all they gave us was a very quizzical look. I really think that in their opinion we were crackers. But nevertheless the performance was a great success. We haven't taken any professional bookings yet, but we are ever hopeful.

All too soon the week was coming to an end. To be able to spend seven days with friends and business partners, enjoying work and play is very therapeutic.

The last day dawned. We spent our time, shopping for tourist items to take home, packing, lazing by the pool and talking through the exploits of the week.

The evening was a banquet and ball, with at last, the opportunity to wear our best clothes and say our farewells to Sicily.

In my capacity as President, I was seated on the top table, with the Godfather one side of me and my husband the other. After a most sumptuous dinner and a comfort break, the band arrived to help us finish the week in style. I love dancing so I couldn't keep still for long. The Godfather asked me if I would do him the honour of dancing with him from time to time throughout the evening. Of course I said that I would be delighted and that it would be an honour. I happened to be a bit taller in my high heel shoes than he was, so when he clasped me to him, his nose was in my cleavage next to my chain of office. I can imagine that there are not many women who can boast about this. So as not to embarrass him any further I kicked off my shoes and threw them under the top table. That was much better; I could now look him in the eyes. It was very hot, so I decided to dance bear foot for the rest of the evening. At the stroke of midnight we all took our partners for the obligatory 'last waltz'.

Saying good night to all, I fished under the table for my shoes. To my surprise they were no longer there. I didn't worry about this too much. I felt that if that was all I had lost in one fabulous week, it was a small price to pay.

Early the next morning after finishing the packing, the coaches arrived to take us to the airport. The cases were loaded and so were we. The Godfather came in his staff car to the airport not only to help me through the customs with all my excess baggage, but I think, to make sure we all left *his* Island.

Once all safely aboard, the Godfather came onto the plane to say goodbye. I thanked him profusely for looking after us and gave him a small present to commemorate our visit. He in turn thanked us all for visiting Sicily and giving him an insight into British sense of humour. He took my hand, kissed it, and then handed me a present, which I was made to unwrap in front of him.

It was my dance shoes. I think he was trying to emulate our humour. It left something out in the translation but we felt that we should all laugh or else we might not leave the tarmac.

Two weeks after arriving home Mount Etna blew quite badly. I was very glad to be in England, and not in Sicily.

THE MAGNIFICENT TEN

L ife can be dreary unless you look for excitement.

During my days whilst still in Business, I was asked if I would like to travel to Canada with nine male Ironmongers, hereafter known as "Guys" (Canadian terminology for both sexes), to study Home Hardware Canada. Similar in size if not bigger than Asda in England.

Rumours that I shared the men on a rota system are purely jealous gossip. I'm sorry to say they all behaved like the "True British Gentlemen that they were".

I had never been on a trip alone before with all men. I thought, this could prove to be exciting.

From Gatwick we flew over Newfoundland, down the St. Lawrence waterway to land in Toronto. It was a good flight, lots of food, drink, good company and Ironmonger chat.

On going through customs, I was the only person searched. It was probably something to do with the fact that I had nine male partners, or so they thought. Eventually outside, we boarded the Holiday Inn bus to take us to the hotel.

The next day dawned very wet and windy, typical British weather really. We spent the day in downtown Toronto spying out the local opposition.

The next hitch was due to all the walking as I had now put my toe right through my tights. Everything had to come to a standstill while I tried to buy a new pair.

I was accompanied by all nine men as we visited a store suitable for my requirements. On asking the assistant for a pair of tights, she went into convulsive laughter and said, "Do you mean the sort that male ice hockey players wear?" I delicately pointed out that I was not a male ice hockey player and showed her my dilemma. "Oh", she said, trying hard to stifle a giggle, "You mean pantyhose". Having at last solved this international crisis we went on our way visiting more and more Hardware Stores.

En route we sampled the local ice creams, sundaes, hamburgers and we watched cookies being made and still it was pouring with rain.

It wasn't long before we had another crisis on our hands. Our leader Ken had forgotten to pack his swimming trunks. Being true friends and Ironmongers we all decided to help him buy a new pair. This we thought would be an easy task. It's surprising how wrong you can be sometimes. Every store we visited seemed to sell only the bikini type and for ladies. I think the shop assistant was more embarrassed than Ken. After much deliberation our leader is now the proud owner of a very saucy pair of trunks.

Later, after dinner we all met in the hotel pool to see if the trunks did the job they were supposed to. Modesty does not allow me to elaborate.

The piece de resistance was a communal hot soak in the whirlpool. What a smashing way to finish the day.

The following morning we left for Kitchener Waterloo. It was still raining. After lunch a mini bus complete with private chauffeur, arrived to take us to the fall market at a place called Bingham Park.

We were introduced as "The Guys from England". I tactfully pointed out that I was not a "Guy". After some very close inspection, they all agreed.

A full day at the market culminated in being spoilt by the Directors to a very large meal at the Charcoal Steak House, followed by a cabaret with a look alike of Elvis Presley. The steak was good!

In Kitchener Waterloo it is not possible to buy alcohol. I think it is known as a 'dry state'. The English Ironmongers became very upset by this news. Their misery was soon overcome by the marvellous company, good food and pleasant exchanges between Ironmongers.

Monday morning arrived and we attended a working breakfast at 7.00.a.m. By some stroke of genius, we all made it on time. During the meal I sat next to a very interesting gentleman known as 'The Colonel'. His forte was a product called 'Muskol'. This is an insect repellent used by explorers who ride down the Amazon basin trying not to get bitten.

I was made the best offer yet. He said "Come up to my room and see my bugs". These Canadians are sometimes very original.

Two more very large meals later, the day finally came to an end.

There was another working breakfast the next day at 7.00.a.m. I didn't think I could keep up this pace. We British seem to be much more sedentary.

The day was hectic, starting with the fall show at Bingham Park, travelling miles to meet other Hardware men and attending seminars.

The day wound up with a very boring A.G.M. They're bad enough in England when you know the subject matter. In Canada we knew nothing about the finer points being discussed.

Our leader Ken presented the President of Home Hardware Canada with a George IV silver stuffing spoon suitably engraved with the correct initials. Why anyone would want a George IV silver stuffing spoon defeats me, but 'C'est la vie' as they say in the French quarter of Canada.

Back at our hotel we all slumped into the bar for a nightcap, longing for a bit of piece and quiet. No such luck, the band was still playing dance music, so being the only lady I was kept fairly busy. Plumbers and Ironmongers seem to be very light on their toes.

At 1.00.a.m. we received an invitation to attend a party in room 114.

The entertainment was to be by a Newfi, Canadian terminology for a person from Newfoundland. He owned a Hardware store, played the guitar and the harmonica at the same time, and even flew his own aeroplane.

I noticed that in one corner of this room there was a brand new Yamaha guitar. I was told, "You are going to start the entertainment as we know you can play". Panic was beginning to set in here.

I was away from home, and the only lady present. An Ironmonger is flying his own aeroplane in from Newfoundland who not only plays guitar but harmonica as well, and I am expected to start the ball rolling.

I kept away from the guitar as long as I could, hoping that everyone would forget about me. No such luck. The guitar was handed to me and I was asked, "Please start the entertainment". It's at times like this that you wish the ground would open up and swallow you whole. But it never does.

I couldn't think of a thing to play that would be suitable for this occasion. If I could play just one chord, say the chord of D, use an alternating base and not move my left hand on the frets, perhaps I could convince them all that I was a brilliant guitarist.

This method of picking is known as "Till ready". Keep doing this until you are ready and a song springs to mind. The other guitarist said, "Wow, Ann you are a picker". I said, "Yes, but it never gets any better". My Mum always said, "It'll never get better if you pick it".

After picking for a while everyone said, "What are you going to play?" The only thing that came to mind that I could play without moving my left hand was, "A Froggy went a court'n". As this was a Burl Ives number I felt sure they would all know it. Nobody did. I was then asked to teach the other guitarist how to play it. This came as quite a shock to me as I felt that anyone who can not only strum a guitar but blow a tune on a harmonica at the same time must be more brilliant than I ever could be.

During the evening the verses became more colourful. After tumultuous applause, I was asked to play even more. Still without moving my left hand I played, Freres Jacques, Row, Row, Row, your boat, Swing Low Sweet Chariot, Loch Lomond, The Saints, The Runaway Train, Worried Man Blues and finally The Streets of Laredo. I had become a celebrity overnight! We then played some numbers together and a great time was being had by all. At 3.30.a.m. the management received complaints regarding the noise we were making so the party broke up and at long last I crawled into bed.

After only two hours sleep we were attending yet another working breakfast. I had never seen such strange food, eggs and sausages were alright but I wasn't so sure about the green fruit jelly and sticky iced buns.

Throughout the meal we were entertained by a conjuror from Las Vegas. Even at 7.30.a.m. he was very amusing and brilliant.

There must be a reason why I was always being picked on. I think it had something to do with the fact that I was the only English lady Ironmonger, amongst 400 Canadian male Ironmongers. At a given nod from the President, the conjuror approached me asking for help to perform his next illusion. Even though my eggs were going to get cold I could not refuse. He asked me to open my hand into which he placed a red soft ball.

Whilst he performed more tricks, I was made to keep my hand very tightly clenched and not to open it. I could still not eat my breakfast, much to everyone's amusement. Nearly five minutes later he approached me again, made me stand up and open my hand for all to see. Out popped not one red ball, but three. I still to this day cannot work out how this was done. Perhaps it could be something to do with compression and heat.

Now, I thought, breakfast. Wrong for two reasons, firstly it was now stone cold and secondly I was asked to take the platform and talk to these 400 Ironmongers about life in England. This was 'off the cuff'. I had never done this before. I think my bravado took over at this point as when I had finished, some 15 minutes had elapsed. As there was no breakfast left I went hungry.

I had now been introduced to public speaking, in a way that I had never dreamed of, but I loved it. There was to be no going back from now on.

After breakfast, the morning was spent in downtown Kitchener Waterloo visiting more Hardware stores. The evening found us in the 'Corkscrew eating house' sampling more steaks. We don't have such lovely sounding names of restaurants in England.

In the elevator on the way to our rooms that night, there were English and Canadian Ironmongers. I said in a fairly loud clear voice, "Will you all please knock me up early in the morning". I didn't know then what I know now. As you can imagine I had my leg pulled unmercifully. In the morning there were some very strange notices hanging on my bedroom doorknob.

In the morning we were taken to a factory to watch them make files and pliers. Just think, we have travelled all the way to Canada to watch men make files. Life can be exciting at times can't it? We had to be up very early to be collected ready for the long drive to Port Hope, on Lake Ontario.

We made our way to the Nicholson File Plant to watch this exciting piece of work in progress. I can now admit that the visit was very different from anything I had ever seen before, very noisy but fascinating nevertheless. The skill and the speed of the professional tool makers was remarkable. Conversation was impossible as we all wore ear defenders. The constant pounding of hydraulic hammers was painful.

At the end of the tour we were given a file, hot off the production line, and I do mean hot. A toy red London Transport bus, which was a replica of the one used on an advertising campaign in England.

On leaving the factory there was just enough time left to visit more Hardware Stores before being treated once again for another steak at the Charcoal House restaurant.

By now, most of us were finding it difficult to move as we felt that we must have consumed at least a whole cow each. Dancing in the bar seems to be a good way of trying to burn off the excess food.

Boy…Living this lifestyle is very hard work.

When the next day dawned, to our surprise, the sun was shining for the first time during the trip. Our driver Rik, came to take us to the Home Hardware distribution centre at St. Jacobs. Everything was operated by computers, which we thought at the time was a very new fangled idea.

It took all morning just to see around the centre. Everything seemed to be so much bigger in Canada than in England. I began to feel like the poor relative.

After lunch we were taken to the boardroom for a meeting. The boardroom table probably cost more than all my stock put together. The table was highly polished and stretched the entire length of the boardroom. I leant my elbows on this wonderful piece of wood and promptly fell asleep, I think jet lag was catching up here, or it could be all the food. The only thing that woke me up was when my elbows slid off the very shiny table. It took me a long time to live that down.

Saturday arrived, wet, windy and bitterly cold. This was the worst weather Canada had experienced for 50 years. We had decided to visit Niagara Falls.

After enquiring at the reception desk about transport, we were given the number of a Mother who took bookings for her son a taxi driver. The clerk telephoned her for us, and told her of our plans and how many passengers there would be. In less than half an hour our taxi arrived.

The driver said he would spend the entire day with us. The cost to be divided between the four passengers was $20 each. Quite reasonable we thought.

After a fast hair-raising journey of some two and a half hours we arrived at Niagara Falls, surely one of the great wonders of the world. The weather was still appalling. We were by now so wet that we decided to go all the way and take a trip on the "Maid of the Mists boat" into Horseshoe Falls. We asked our driver to join us at our expense, but we could not understand why he declined our generous offer.

Before boarding the boat we were issued with full length, hooded black Macs. This was a very good disguise as it was now impossible to distinguish one person from another. The 'Guys' disowned me at this point as I had a fit of the giggles. I told them that they looked like monks in dirty habits. A bit weak, but I thought it was funny then.

The ride was very frightening but exciting. The force of the water hit the rocks, then the deck of the boat and finally splashed up underneath the Macs and made us wetter. The stinging water hitting your eyes at speed made it impossible to take a photograph.

Once into Horseshoe falls as far as we could go due to the force of water, we were asked to hold tightly to the grab rail, the pilot was now about to turn the boat around and try to get back from whence we came. The boat seemed to tip over too far for comfort. It's at times like this that a few prayers are said, hoping that the engine will not fail now. Fortunately for us all the engine was still running as we completed the turn. It is also impossible to speak and be heard above the noise of Falls.

When we arrived back safely to the docking area, discarding the proverbial Macs, that's when we realised how wet we all were. Our trusty driver was there to meet us and we told him that we needed a call of nature before the next part of the expedition. On arriving at the Ladies, I tried to dry my hair and some of my clothes. There was a very efficient hand drier available, so I put my head underneath this and slowly dried out whilst getting warmer.

Our next adventure we hoped was to ride in the overhead cable car above the whirlpool. The weather was now so severe that this facility was closed due to safety precautions. The cable car was swaying precariously over the whirlpool. In one way I was pleased that it was cancelled, but the exhilaration would have been tremendous.

The town of Niagara to me is very similar to Las Vegas, a lot colder though, no sand but very noisy and brash. I was now convinced that we had experienced the Falls at the best time, the weather was so foul we were the only people there.

We discovered while there that the Falls recede one inch every year and that in winter the water freezes to a depth of seventy feet.

Just to help us get the blood flowing once again we visited the waxworks. Standing in the queue to pay the entrance fee, I noticed some wax models, they were so lifelike, I even said "Good afternoon". As you can imagine they were very rude and didn't reply.

Making our way up the tremendous double staircase there were two attendants waiting who we thought were there to direct us. The person in front of me actually asked this man for advice. At first there was no reply and we all assumed he was made of wax. Just as we walked away he grabbed one of us by the arm and said, "This way please". Some screamed but most of us collapsed with laughter. We had all been had, well and truly.

After finishing the tour of the waxworks our taxi driver then took us to his favourite workman's café for home made blueberry pie and coffee, which he insisted on paying for. We decided not to argue. All the drivers wanted to talk to us as we were English and loved to hear our strange accent.

Back at the hotel and after a very warming bath we were taken out yet again to the Great West Beef Co. Again for dinner we were served another half a cow, or it could have been a bull.

The next day I decided to lie in bed and came down for breakfast at lunch time. Now recuperated I felt ready for the next bit of fun.

This was a visit to an eighteenth century pioneer village at a town called Doon. It was fascinating to see how the early settlers managed without the modern amenities that we all now enjoy.

In complete contrast the evening was spent in a very modern home of one of our Canadian friends, where we took their home comforts for granted.

You may get the impression that all we did was play. That is not true, we worked very hard as well visiting more and more Hardware stores, some enormous but many in local farming communities.

Our fun for another evening was in the home of one of our Canadian friends, where they gave us a fabulous party in their underground den. The husband played the drums, I played the guitar and one member of our British party owned up that he too could play the drums. There are times when Ironmongers have hidden talents. I tried unsuccessfully to play the drums but I couldn't get both hands and feet co-ordinated, even when a friend put his hand on one knee to keep the alternating beat the other one moved at the same time. I know when I am defeated.

After breakfast the next day we were driven to a village called Dayton. This was a farming community with a large settlement of Menanites. A horse and buggy are the means of transport, everyone is dressed in black and the men have beards. I felt that I had stepped back in time 150 years. It's very difficult to imagine how these people live so simply in a very progressive country.

At the other end of the scale I came across the local blacksmith and became fascinated by his workshop and what he was doing. He saw my look of interest and invited me in to take a closer look. At first I was impressed that I should even be spoken to, and then my feelings soon dissipated. It became clear that he didn't get many visitors as he would not stop talking about his life as a blacksmith and what a pleasure it was to talk to some 'Real English People'.

It took me nearly forty five minutes to escape from his clutches, it was not easy escaping from a very large muscle bound blacksmith.

There are some lovely sounding names of towns in Canada, the next stop was Elmire. It sounds more rural than Tooting Broadway.

The next exciting stop was at the Waterloo County stock yards. How the folks understand what the auctioneer says defeats me. I did learn a few lessons though. I am now the proud owner of two heifers, one hog and one old work horse.

It was now the turn of the English Ironmongers to foot the bill and treat all our Canadian business friends to a slap up meal. I believe some speeches were made, but most of them were unintelligible as the wine was flowing copiously. The energy that Canadian Ironmongers seem to have was becoming impossible to keep up with.

One whole day was spent in the distribution centre at St. Jacobs. We were given an insight into the planning stages of their next advertising campaign followed by a very large lunch and a visit to the computer room. This room was bigger than my store in England. The fun had still not finished.

Our driver called Orvie took us to the Holiday Inn downtown

Toronto in the heart of China Town. This was another new experience for me. The Chinese food was some of the best I had ever tasted.

After satisfying our appetites yet again, some of the "Guys" decided to go to the top of the C.N.Tower which is one fifth of a mile high, and the tallest free standing building in the world at that time. The view from the top at night was breathtaking. Our driver took the men somewhere else. I think it was a bar with topless waiters and dancers, women, I hasten to add.

By the next day it was no longer raining, the sun was shining but it was still bitterly cold. Toronto is knee deep in Hardware stores and I think I visited every one before the day was out. That night we were treated to another enormous meal by the Red Devils Incorporated. I thought they might have been aerobatic pilots but no, they made tools.

We all too soon realised that our adventure was coming to an end, so we held a meeting to determine what we had learnt and how we could put this knowledge to good use once back home.

On our last evening we spent all our remaining dollars on a Japanese meal. We were seated in a circle around a metal table with a big hole at its centre. This is where our chef was standing. His name was AOKI so we called him A.O.K. Rice wine was served in what looked like a specimen vase, even the taste was debateable. We ordered shrimps, steak mushrooms onions and bean shoots. AOKI produced an enormous knife and pretended to threaten us, but luckily he topped, tailed and sliced the shrimps faster than the eye could see. He sprinkled salt all over us to make sure we tasted O.K. and then threw the bean shoots about four feet into the air before they settled into our bowls. He was a good shot. Each table had its own chef who stayed with you all evening, cooking and entertaining. A truly wonderful last night.

Our last day in Canada had arrived where we all went our separate ways to buy the proverbial pressies for the folks back home.

My last thoughts of this unusual two weeks were how to say thank you to all "The Guys" who looked after this one lady Ironmonger.

So thanks to the following:-

To Guy Number one.	The best dance partner.
To Guy Number two.	Who told me that after a very expensive hair

cut I didn't look a day over twenty one.

To Guy Number three. For knocking on my door every morning.

To Guy Number four. For looking after me in China Town.

To Guy Number five. For taking me to the top of the C.N.Tower.

To Guy Number six. For always being cheerful.

To Guy Number seven. For never being tired.

To Guy Number eight. For being a sport.

To Guy Number nine. Our leader and Mother hen for making sure we were always in the right place at the right time.

Without him this adventure would not have been possible.

SEA SICK IN THE SINAI

I announced to my family and friends that I was about to embark on an adventure in the Sinai desert, to live with the Bedouin, and ride a camel all day, I would be sleeping under the stars with no tent, no water for washing and no toilet facilities.

Their immediate response was that as camels have a very unusual gait, throwing your body backwards and forwards will automatically cause travel sickness. I told them all emphatically that as I was an experienced horse rider, this would present no problem to me at all. I hoped.

This was yet another dream of mine about to come true. I have always wanted to experience life in the desert and to escape from the modern world, even if it would only be for one week.

A few years before this adventure took place, I was lucky enough to visit the Sinai desert for one day with my sister and one of my disabled clients, a tetraplegic, as a result of a sporting accident.

During the week we spent our time scuba diving and snorkelling on the coral reef in the Red Sea.

This entire trip had been organised by a group called Back Up, enabling amputees and people with physical disabilities to engage in sports.

On our last day we decided to look at the world above sea level and visit the Sinai desert. On asking around for help we finally located two Bedouin who, for a fee, would take the three of us where we wanted to go.

A very dirty dilapidated four by four arrived outside our Hotel. This was to be our first class transportation for the day.

The truck had no door on the passenger side and the interior was even dirtier than the exterior. With help from both the very strong Bedouin, my disabled client was lifted into the vehicle. This is where the next minor problem occurred. There were no seat belts. This didn't bother the Bedouin or my sister and I, but I had to keep my disabled friend in his seat, as he has no control over balance. Luckily, I don't know why, but I had packed a long length of very soft rope, just in case. My Girl Guide skills were now coming to the fore. So, after applying a half hitch, a granny knot and a few prayers the job was completed.

As we entered the desert, two armed guards stopped the vehicle and a fairly heated exchange took place. Our guide told us to keep absolutely quiet and not to utter one word in English. I don't know what was said but after nearly five minutes of verbal exchange, we were allowed through.

We enjoyed the day including the heat, the sand, the dust, and the silence. The vastness, beauty and tranquility was staggering. Even the goat stew was a first for me.

The meat and vegetables were washed in the oasis as we watched. This was life I had wanted to experience.

After a snooze one of the Bedouin took us for a walk. He showed us *his* palm tree in the oasis, explaining that no one else would pick the dates, only his family members as his father was the chief of the particular Bedouin tribe. Throughout the entire day we saw some wild life but no other human beings, making me realise how easy it would be to become lost and disorientated without the help of the very friendly local people.

By now I was hooked and started searching for the vehicle to help me realise this dream. Through an acquaintance I was given the name of a firm called Wind, Sand and Stars. I surfed the net, as you do, and finally made contact.

After many phone calls I booked a trip called a Sinai Retreat. This was a three day camel trek with four days walking and exploring the desert. I would be living with the Bedouin, with no tent you just put your bed roll down wherever you happen to be. There would be no toilet facilities as we know them and no water for washing; just for drinking.

The next job was to make sure I had the correct gear to enable me to fit in and survive this expedition. The clothing was first on my list. Thin cotton trousers with plenty of pockets, large cotton T-shirts, large being the operative word here, to enable your body to breathe. I needed a safari hat, a Kfir, long sleeved shirts, a bandana, a holdall and a survival bag. A survival bag is made of very strong plastic and is coloured bright orange. I enquired as to why I needed this piece of equipment and was told that should you get lost or become injured, crawl inside the bag and stay there. Once it is realised that you are lost, the helicopters will search for you, notice the bag, which is easily seen from the air and your rescue will be imminent.

The first aid kit needed to contain sun block, chap stick, bite cream, rehydration powders, Savlon, plasters and of course sea sick tablets, which I felt I would not need. I knew I would be too worried about the camel, the snakes, the scorpions, the sand storms, no toilet and no washing to even think of feeling sick.

The washing gear was very meagre, wet wipes for face and hands, plus different ones for the other end. Nappy sacks were needed for your personal rubbish, as anything non bio-degradable must not be left in the desert.

A few nagging doubts crept in from time to time. How will I survive this ordeal with no tent, no toilets and no privacy except perhaps the nearest rock or a sparse bush?

Some equipment, I was lucky enough to borrow from a friend. This included an arctic sleeping bag and mat, a wind proof and waterproof jacket, a small back pack and two elastic bungee straps. I wasn't sure why I needed a waterproof jacket, I didn't think it rained in the desert.

Then I checked that all my vaccinations were current, for example, Hepatitis A, Typhoid, Tetanus and Polio. My passport was current, my holiday insurance updated and now at last I felt ready.

I arrived in Sharm-el-Sheikh at about 10.15.p.m. local time in a very small, almost empty aeroplane. Already this was nothing like arriving at Gatwick. I saw a courier with the name of Wind, Sand and Stars on a board and I hurriedly made myself known.

There were eight other passengers on the plane who would be taking part in this adventure. Once we were all assembled, the courier took us outside the airport to a very dirty and dusty four by four, into which we all climbed.

Our luggage was unceremoniously thrown onto the roof rack and secured with yards of rope. The smell inside the vehicle was indescribable, but not to be down hearted we did our best to remain cheerful, talkative and polite.

For some two and a half hours we sped into the night. I couldn't see where we were going but I hoped our trusty driver could. I knew it was dark in the desert without a moon but this was something I hadn't bargained for. Suddenly without any warning the vehicle did a very sharp right hand turn, followed by a severe bump and we were now in the Sinai desert at 1.00.a.m. I was just beginning to realise how cold it can get.

After a very short distance the driver stopped, got out of the truck to engage the four by four onto the wheels then let some air out of the tyres to enable the vehicle to travel across sand and rocks.

The terrain was very bumpy and very dark. One minute we were on rocks the next we were stuck in soft sand. Only the driver and the courier were allowed to help at this point. We were told that it was too dangerous for mere novices to get out of the truck at this stage. I was beginning to wonder what I had let myself in for.

The good side was that there was a new moon and more stars than I had ever seen before. The sky was so clear and there seemed to be more of it than in England. No pollution means clearer skies. But clearer skies mean colder weather at night. As the heat dissipates and rises there are no clouds to stop it escaping.

We eventually arrived at our first camp site in a canyon surrounded by Bedouin and four other tourists all fast asleep in the open. It was very dark, quite cold and very creepy. My saving grace was, as I could not see what might be crawling in the sand that might bite me, perhaps I shouldn't worry too much. After the four by four was unloaded we really enjoyed some well deserved hot soup.

I asked our guide, "Where do I sleep?" His reply was a gem, he said, "Madam you have the whole of the Sinai desert to choose from, take your pick". Cheeky devil I thought.

I needed some help to find a suitable bit of sand. I can assure you that it is not as soft as it looks. There are buried rocks everywhere. To try to unwrap your bed roll and sleeping bag whilst trying to find something warm to wear is not easy at 2.00.a.m. in a very dark cold desert. The bed mat is a vital piece of equipment as this keeps the cold from entering your body at night.

I finally succeeded in laying out the bed mat, untied the sleeping bag and found something suitable like a very warm track suit, my woolly bobble hat, thick socks and gloves to sleep in. If a good looking young Bedouin had tried to take advantage of me I think I would have frightened him off women for life.

As you can imagine after the cold and then the hot soup mixed with a few nerves and excitement, a call of nature was desperately needed. I was a bit worried and confused, so I asked for advice. "Choose anywhere you like, there is no one to watch you," I was told. "Don't go too near any rocks, and if you find a bush, look carefully at any tracks in the sand." By now I was so desperate I didn't really care where I went so long as I could relieve myself. I then had to climb over people fast asleep to disappear into the night to find a suitable spot to do what a girl needs to do.

Finally much relieved I made it safely back to my bed roll and crawled inside, taking with me a lot of unwanted sand but at last beginning to get warm. I had never felt so alone before, but strangely at peace and a little excited.

I didn't get much sleep on this my first night for a number of reasons.

Firstly, the time was now 2.30.a.m. and we had to get up at 6.00.a.m.

I was very cold and the sand was not as soft as I had been led to believe. All the time I was in my bag I constantly tried to wiggle my bottom into a hollow. After a very short time this hollow became very hard. Already, even after only one night, my hips were bruised.

By 6.00.a.m I was ready to get up, but so was everyone else. There is no privacy at all. Casting caution to the wind I sat on my bed roll took one set of clothes off and put another lot on, making sure there was nothing in them that I wouldn't like to spend the day with. Of course by now there was sand in everything. I do mean everything.

Everyone seemed to disappear into the unknown at once. Women went left and men went right.

As we were being hurried, there was only time to use a wet wipe on the face and hands and not even enough time to clean my teeth. Why should I worry, who would notice? I was now covered in sand and sweat, I didn't know where any of my clothes were and I was tired, thirsty and hungry.

Before starting breakfast we were all given our own mug for tea. This is your responsibility to keep it with you all the time, no matter where you go and to make sure that it's kept clean.

Placed in the sand are three bowls of water. Clean your hands first with alcohol gel and rinse off in bowl number one. Bowl number two contains Dettol; this is for washing your mug. Bowl number three is for rinsing same with clean water.

From now on, all food is consumed as nature intended. As there is nothing to dry the mug or your hands with, you just stand there and shake and the sun does the rest.

Breakfast was served at 7.00.am.consisting of Bedouin tea made in a large old tin kettle placed on an open fire. There are no cows around so this is served black, and it was very good and tasty. Sugar was available, but it never looked very clean as it was always near the fire.

Twenty four boiled eggs, still with the shells on arrived in a very large bowl, giving us two each as there were twelve of us in total. This was a do-it-yourself job. Fresh baked unleavened bread which had been cooked in the fire was not my cup of tea, but, if you're hungry anything will do. Once you have knocked the ash off it's quite palatable.

After breakfast, the temperature was steadily rising. It was a great feeling to get some warmth into my body but what I didn't know was just how hot it was going to get.

We were all told to start packing up the night gear as the camels and more Bedouin would be arriving shortly.

How to pack the clothes into my rucksack without too much sand was definitely not an easy task. I then tried to get the sleeping bag back into its outer bag. I had never done this before so with a lot of help and advice from the other travellers I succeeded. As I stuffed all my gear back into the holdall, the zip broke. My entire belongings are now open to the elements and creatures of the desert. The guide suggested that everything be put into my survival bag and held in place with my two bungee straps. You see, I knew they would be useful one day. My Mum always told me to be prepared.

This was only the first morning, things could only get better, I hoped.

Once breakfast was finished and the bags finally packed, the Bedouin and camels arrived, to take us to our next camp. Each of us were assigned our own camel and our own cameleer.

I loaded my back pack with survival kit, water, sun block, wet wipes and just to be on the safe side, lots more water. I applied sun block to all the parts of my body which could be exposed to the burning sun, put on my safari hat and bandana around my neck and tied my sunglasses on. We were advised to tuck trousers into the top of your socks. This prevented my legs being burnt and luckily stopped anything crawling into parts of my body.

Once we all announced our readiness the guide gave us a briefing regarding the amount of water needed to consume every day. How important it is to remain covered at all times, watch out for snakes, scorpions and anything that might bite. I knew this was going to be an adventure.

For the next thirty five minutes we walked behind the camels due to the fact that the terrain was too steep to ride. This made me realise how valuable the camels are to the Bedouin. Tourists might be cheap but their camels are their livelihood.

Upon reaching more level terrain it was now time to get mounted. The saddle on the first camel they gave me was too small to fit my bottom, so a larger one was immediately found. Getting onto a camel is quite fun and easy, providing he is sitting down. I was now astride my camel and raring to go. What a shock as the camel then stands. I was firstly thrown forwards and when I felt that I was going to fall off, I was then thrown backwards until all four legs were touching the sand. I'm glad to say that only the camels legs were in this position, I was still on board.

Me and my camel on three day trek in the Sinai desert

As there are no stirrups on a camels' saddle, after a while both legs suffer pins and needles and then go numb. I asked the guide how to overcome this problem and was told to cross one leg over the other at the front of the saddle, hooking one foot behind the other and when one leg has come back to life, change legs.

I felt like Laurence of Arabia, riding off into the sunset.

After about one hour, riding at a steady pace, the temperature is now reaching something quite frightening, but the experience was exciting and somewhat exhilarating. The vast areas of sand and wilderness are beyond description and it made me feel very small and a bit vulnerable.

I thought the expression, "Everything stops for tea", was purely a British phenomena, but no, it appears to be universal. The Bedouin found the only shade available for miles around.

Trying to get about fifteen people under a very small tree is not an easy task, but with skill and patience, all things are possible. A fire was made and the kettle began to sing. I never knew that a cuppa could be so delicious.

The minute I stepped out from the shelter of the tree I became very aware of how important just a little bit of shade could be.

The next task was to find a suitable bit of privacy to answer a call of nature. I was told how important it was to tell the Bedouin where you were going to enable them to check the ground for tracks in the sand.

As long as they knew where you were, should anything go wrong, they would know where to find you. The thoughts of squatting on a scorpion, made me shudder. How embarrassing if you were bitten there.

After a cup of tea and a wee, we mounted the camels again and headed for the next stop and lunch.

By now it was nearly midday and temperatures soared. It's surprising how the heat makes you feel. For me I was getting tired as well as hungry and very thirsty, even though I had already consumed two litres of water. Finding somewhere in the shade was not easy this time.

Our guide informed us that we would be better off up the mountain under an overhang, rather than spend a lot of valuable time looking for another tree.

Climbing a small mountain with loose shale in the heat of the day was almost more than I could manage. Being the most mature person in the party, it took me a bit longer, but with all the verbal encouragement from the younger folk who had made it to the top, I too finally made it.

I never realised that sitting on hard rocks in the shade could be so wonderful.

Once we were all safely in the shade, the Bedouin then had to carry all the food up the mountain. We just panted and sat there watching, they were obviously more used to this heat than we were.

A very welcome lunch of tomatoes, halva, cucumber, sweet corn, baked beans, tuna, cheese, unleavened bread, crisps and finally a cup of tea were served. Well, not exactly served. All the above mentioned food was laid on a flat bed of rocks and then we were told, help yourself. Balancing up a mountain overhang, grabbing the food in one hand and hanging on with the other was something I had never tried to do before.

After lunch, we were told to find a niche in the mountain and grab an hour's sleep. This was the most painful sleep I had ever experienced.

I had bruises in places were bruises shouldn't be.

Well refreshed, we made our way back down the mountain, mounted the camels and rode to the retreat campsite where we would stay for five nights.

Suddenly from out of nowhere we were hit by a sandstorm. The force of sand hitting your face at speed is just like having a facial scrub. The sand goes up your nose, in your eyes and ears and anywhere it can get. It then sticks to the sweat on your skin. We very quickly dismounted the camels and sheltered in the lea of the mountain all huddled together with our backs to the wind. The cameleers held on very tightly to their charges. Once this storm had passed through we mounted up again and finally

made it to the camp site, looking, I hasten to add, rather dirty and sandy. I then tried with my wet wipes to get clean. This proved to be an impossible task, so I gave up and decided to stay dirty.

Dinner was served at 7.00.p.m consisting of pasta and salad. Well I think that's what it was. In the desert there is no dusk, just day or night. Day starts at about 5.00a.m and night descends at about 6.00.p.m. Sometimes I was thankful for darkness as you cannot see what you are eating.

By 8.30.p.m. we were all tired and ready for bed. There is nothing to do, no radio and no television. I didn't miss civilisation one jot.

To sleep where you stop and just put your bed roll down is quite something. If I am honest I felt a little afraid and somewhat alone as we were all widely scattered around this big canyon. The good side is that as it's so dark no one can see you undress and as we are all so far apart no one can see you reverse the process in the morning. I hoped.

By 6.00a.m the next morning I was wide awake, but unfortunately so were the damn flies. The desert was experiencing a plethora of these buzzing creatures, completely out of season. I'm now not only covered in sand but flies as well. As fast as I swiped them off me, they were back again. Finally I got used to them crawling all over me, unless they were somewhere unacceptable.

Before taking myself off to the private area set aside for ladies, it was very important that the sleeping bag was folded over and weighed down with rocks to prevent anything crawling inside.

After a walk into the mountain area for the en-suite facilities I used a wet wipe on my face and hands and then cleaned my teeth, the first time for two days. It was a wonderful feeling.

Feeling a little more refreshed I sat on my sleeping bag, removed my night clothes and donned my desert outfit. As I rolled up my bed roll, a very large black beetle crawled out. He didn't bite me so I didn't bite him. As he toddled off into the sandy yonder I tickled his bum which made him crawl even faster. I called him Paul or Ringo.

The only other type of wild life I had seen so far included, would you believe, pigeons, martins, swallows and migrating eagles who were so high they were barely visible. I had seen goats, camels and beautiful transparent white lizards.

As I started to pack up my bedroll I noticed some very strange footprints surrounding the area where I had slept. On asking a Bedouin what is was, he said, "Don't worry it was only a desert fox checking to see if you were edible". He obviously thought I wasn't, as I am still alive and kicking.

The breakfast was good, but very different to anything I had ever tasted. We were served Falafel, unleavened bread and a strange milky drink a bit like a cereal containing nuts and muesli. It was so filling that I could only drink one cup full and then my appetite was satisfied. This was followed by more black tea to wash everything down.

The morning was spent doing our own thing. I chose to wander off into the desert to explore. Before leaving the camp area I was advised to tell the Bedouin roughly where I was going and how long I planned to be away. It was important to make a mental note of the shapes of certain rocks so that in the event of becoming lost and providing I can see the exact same shape rock, I will make it safely back to camp. It's very hard to explain what it's like to feel completely alone in the Sinai desert. It's so quiet, vast and beautiful but a little nerve racking. I obviously made it safely back to camp.

The rest of the morning was spent trying to remain in the shade and read my book. I found some shade in the lea of the mountain area, but unfortunately so did the damn flies. As the sun moved round so did I to chase the shade every ten to fifteen minutes. This tranquillity was finally broken by the announcement that lunch was ready.

For the afternoon the Bedouin had planned a two hour walk into the desert, to visit an enormous rock with a hole right through it. The nearest thing to a tourist attraction I think. To get to this rock and out of the camp we all had to climb over an enormous sand dune, the sort you see in movies. Trust me they do exist.

To reach the summit was one of the hardest things I had ever done.

Being, as I have said, the most senior person in the party, I was the last one to make it to the top. It didn't help having two arthritic knees.

Once or twice I nearly admitted defeat. As I put one step forward, my foot disappeared into the sand and I not only slid sideways but backwards as well. By the time I had moved the other foot forward I was further back than I was before I started. With a lot of encouragement from the rest of the group, I finally made it. I was now so hot and bothered that the thoughts of going on began to trouble me just a bit. I began to feel disheartened.

Throughout the two hour walk in the heat of the day we experienced even more flies and winds so strong that we had to walk backwards just to remain standing. On reaching the rock, I was too exhausted to climb to the top, as to get there you had to crawl up another enormous sand dune. All the younger fitter bodies made it to the top while I waited at the bottom to get a photo of everyone jumping on to the sand dune the other side and sliding down.

According to the Bedouin we were now experiencing other phenomena in the shape of extreme humidity, low cloud and poor visibility, not what to expect in the desert, England yes, but Sinai, no.

I needed two people to help me walk, one on each arm and lots of verbal encouragement pacing me one step at a time. One half of the party went ahead to warn the Bedouin of my problem whilst I was left with just my two stalwarts to get me back to camp. Nearly three hours later the camp came in to view. I was never so pleased to see *home*.

I was made to lay in the shade whilst water was poured all over me to try to get my body temperature down. Two litres of water disappeared down my throat without touching the sides. It was nearly two hours before I felt good enough to stand up and thank my helpers for getting me back to camp.

I think throughout that day I had not drunk as much as I should have done, so I suffered the consequences. I became very overheated, nauseas, giddy and totally exhausted. I really began to understand how easy it would have been to give up. I just wanted to drop down on my knees, cry and go to sleep.

What an exciting week it was turning out to be.

My body and my clothes were filthy, I was covered in sand, my holdall had broken, and my sleeping mat had a slow puncture. I had been visited at night by a desert fox, spent the night with a beetle, been buzzed by a mosquito, covered in flies, and one morning I even counted three drops of rain.

I bet you are all jealous of my good fortune. The good side, I didn't meet a scorpion and I only saw the tracks of a deadly viper. This is a bonus because should I get bitten there are only four hours to get the ante-venom into your system or else it's goodbye Annie.

I think the evening meal, served at 7.00.p.m was probably chicken. I'm not sure, but it tasted good. What I missed was a pudding; this luxury doesn't happen in the desert. I also missed not having a cup of coffee only black tea to wash everything down. Weight Watchers eat your heart out.

The evenings were spent sitting on carpets made from camel hair, covered in sand, chatting round the fire, being taught Bedouin games played in the sand and watching the shooting stars.

Every morning at about 3.00.a.m. we would all wake up just to watch the Milky Way travel overhead. I had never seen this before. What a sight!

The Bedouin are a lovely race of people, kind and caring, thoughtful and very good cooks. The women seem, in my opinion to do the hard work, and the men do the cooking and washing up.

Every morning at 5.00.a.m. the wife of Kordish, our chef, walked into the desert alone, looking for kindling to make the fire, which is kept going all day long. One morning when I could no longer sleep I arose and helped the wife collect the kindling. Whilst she was breaking the dried wood with her hands she winced in pain. I grabbed her hand and she showed me her very torn fingers which were split, cracked and bleeding.

I went to my first aid kit and gave her my whole pack of plasters, a tube of Savlon and a tube of hand cream. You would have thought that I had given her the crown jewels. This brought home to me how very basic their life in the desert could be.

Our guide Amra was a young Egyptian employed by the travel agent to be our interpreter. He spoke perfect English; and a mere 28 years old, he was young, strong and very good looking.

As stated earlier this trip was called a retreat. Being honest, I didn't know what that was. I thought it just meant a retreat into the desert to get away from the world for a few days. I was wrong. It is a religious retreat led by a Reverend. This might cause me a few problems as I am not religious and only go to church for weddings and funerals.

I knew, initially, I would find this hard to come to terms with. There are times of day when silence must be observed. How could I possibly keep my mouth shut during this period?

At 7.00.a.m. every morning before breakfast, a service took place in the Bedouin tent which lasted for just thirty minutes. I was invited on many occasions to participate, but after declining their offer they finally realised that, "I could not be saved".

To hear English prayers and hymns wafting across the Sinai every morning, somehow didn't seem right to me, but I was very happy to let the others do, what to them, was an important part of their day. I might not have a religion, but I respect others who have.

This time of day, I then decided was mine. As I couldn't speak to anyone for at least thirty minutes I took myself off into the desert for some private ablutions. I was not always alone at this time of day, as the tour operator shared some of my thoughts. We would sit together in the shade, whispering and putting the world to rights.

On one particular occasion on a long desert walk it was voted that no talking would be allowed on the outward journey, only on the way back. I did begin to realise how beautiful the sound of silence could be.

Unfortunately on the outward journey, to get to the start of the walk meant a rather hairy climb. I began to fall and screamed for help. I was immediately asked to keep quiet and not to break the order of silence. How do you scream for help quietly? I was rescued and once safe and secure I kept my trap shut, much to the surprise of everyone.

Every evening at about 8.00 to 8.30.p.m we were all ready for bed.

It was so bright, even with a new moon. The stars were fabulous and it was a joy to lie in the sleeping bag and just stare up at the night sky.

Before leaving home, other travellers told me how cold it gets in the desert at night. During this particular week it turned out not to be true. Only one night out of the seven was cold. The Bedouin told us that the desert was experiencing very unusual weather, not only the flies and high winds but the thick cloud, high humidity and swirling mists.

Why is it, that exciting things seem to follow me wherever I go?

The next day we arose as usual at about 5.30.a.m, followed by tea, prayers, a pretend wash and a visit to the rocks for the en-suite facilities with a fabulous view.

By 9.30.a.m. we were ready for a complete days walk. Today the colour of the sand varied from pale toffee to completely white, mixed with limestone. From a distance it was possible to imagine this was snow. But then who would be stupid enough to think that it can snow in the desert?

After two hours the Bedouin found us some shade, again up a mountain in a crevice which was used by them for storage. This was to be our restaurant for lunch. It consisted of baked beans, feta cheese, and tuna, laughing cow cheeses, sweet corn, halva and the treat of the week melon.

I can't begin to describe what the melon did for my thirst. It was like living on cloud nine.

Two hours later after lunch and a snooze in a tiny hole up a mountain, feeling a little more refreshed we readied ourselves for the two hour walk back to camp.

It was now midday and *a bit warm*. After about one hour of walking I began to feel a little dizzy. I had run out of water and we were not allowed to share drinking vessels. Amra had a new bottle of drinking water in his survival pack which he gave to me to help the situation.

The problem appeared to be that as I had not drunk enough water a few days before, I had not passed any urine for over nine hours. This can cause a major problem.

Back at camp I made up for lost time and drank litre after litre of water to try to put things right.

Dinner that evening was chicken, rice, peppers and tomatoes. I never knew I could enjoy food so much. I was so hungry that I demolished everything I could get my hands on.

During the night, I began to realise how important a loo could be. To make up for my inadequacies of the day, I had to vacate my sleeping bag every thirty minutes throughout the night, find my torch and wander into the desert alone to relieve myself of the pressing problem.

It was very important to check the colour of what is passed. It had to look like white wine not rose. If it's the latter you are in trouble. Trust me, it is not easy at night in the desert to check the colour.

That's another lesson learnt the hard way.

During that fitful sleepless night I moved my bed roll many times to try to find a softer resting place. There seems not to be any.

If only I could paint a picture of the vastness of the Sinai and our sleeping arrangements it would let everyone know how small we are.

The next morning everyone was as usual up and at 'em by 6.00.a.m followed by the usual prayers and hymns, and then breakfast.

I decided to spend the morning writing my diary, reading a book, chasing the shade and swatting the damn flies.

After lunch we were all off for another two hour walk to experience the vastness and wild life, but fortunately no deadly snakes, yet.

On arrival back at the camp, whilst waiting for Kordish to prepare the evening meal, a very loud bang echoed around the canyon. A viper had crawled into the cooking area which Kordish unceremoniously killed with a rock.

Later that day, our camels returned and they were now roaming freely. They were hobbled to prevent them running off into the night. I asked if they had ever trodden on anyone in the dark, they have very big feet and I became a bit worried. I was assured that this had never happened. The early evening was filled with the eerie and noisy sounds that camels make.

At last, I began to settle into this very hard way of life. I wondered what it would be like to have a bath and get rid of all the sand.

That night proved to be the coldest and windiest yet. This is where the arctic sleeping bag came into its own. I never thought it possible to sleep in so many layers of clothes from top to toe. When the sun came up in the morning it was a relief to feel some warmth creep back into your body.

This day was to be a full day riding our camels. After breakfast and the usual routine, we all packed our back packs with the important survival kits. Our guide Amra was to carry an enormous back pack containing spare water bottles and oxygen, plus all the things needed to keep us alive should there be a problem. What a comforting thought!

After an hour and a half camel riding we had to dismount to walk through a very deep gorge. I can only liken it to the Grand Canyon, albeit smaller, but just as dramatic, indescribably steep and very, very hot. Back up again on the camels we rode for another thirty five minutes before finding some shade in Wadi Kerry where lunch was prepared. It was here in this Wadi that I found a 200 million year old snail fossil. It's hard to imagine that at one time this area was once under water and brimming with aquatic life.

My life is never dull as I hope you can see. My next excitement happened that day whilst astride my camel; suddenly a snake reared up in front of me and began to threaten the camel. You can imagine that I called for assistance in a hurry and I was told, "Don't worry it's not a venomous variety. It's only telling you to get off his patch".

We stopped from time to time to rest in the shade and drink water. There was another two hours to ride on the camels before making it back to camp. It is a misconception that deserts are all sand. It's not true. There are vast plains with rocky outcrops, and some trees and bushes, plus mountains and enormous sand dunes. And oh boy is it hot.

Upon nearing our camp we had to dismount as the incline was too steep and too dangerous for the camels to have passengers.

I thought I had seen large sand dunes until this one came into view.

Once or twice I never felt capable of making it to the top. Not only is it difficult to breathe in such intense heat but your mouth becomes dry, your body overheats, you are thirsty and your legs want to collapse. It took me an eternity to get to the top, but I needed lots of verbal encouragement from everyone in the party. Once on top of the dune, getting down the other side was a doddle. Just dig your feet in, sit on your posterior and go. Worry about where the sand is later.

Kordish made us all a genuine cup of Bedouin tea which was so very refreshing and then served dinner.

Each of the twelve tourists was assigned our own cameleer. Mine was the 18-year-old very good looking son of the lady who made the tea every morning. Unfortunately he was born completely deaf as over 7% of the Bedouin are born this way due to intermarrying and genetic disorder. All of the Bedouin use sign language even if they are not deaf.

During my time as a Senior Care Attendant working with my physically disabled clients, some of whom were very deaf, I had studied British Sign Language.

One afternoon whilst sitting around the fire drinking the proverbial cup of tea, I decided that with my small knowledge of sign language I would try to communicate with my cameleer.

I asked him in sign what his name was and then I told him mine. I also asked him if the camel I was riding belonged to him. He replied in sign that yes it was his and that he owned two other camels. I was so excited to think that we could communicate and so was he. No other English tourist had ever tried to communicate with him before. He then got completely carried away as he now thought that I could speak to him at speed. This was not possible so I had to ask him to wait.

To make certain that he had understood our conversation, I asked for the help of Amra our guide and translator. I told him in English what I had asked this young man. He spoke in his native tongue to the boys' Mother, who then spoke in Sign language to her son. Her son then spoke in sign language back to his Mother, who then spoke in her native tongue to our guide who then turned to me and said, "Yes". It took a long time to get an answer, but it was definitely worth it. I sat around the fire with Mum and Son and rabbitted for quite some time, with interjections from Amra. Sometimes I was totally lost and needed help with a translation. I was now made very welcome and treated as one of the family. The effort I had put into this short chat had been worth while.

Eventually, it came to the stage that I had to wash my hair. To do so I had to find a suitable ravine. By using this water ration I was not allowed any more for washing. A girl has to always look her best. Due to the sweat and sand my hair was stiff and standing on end. I felt that I must look like Ken Dodd.

Soon it was our last night in the desert. The following morning, we were all off to visit St. Katharine's monastery, finishing at a Hotel in Sharm-el-Sheikh, to have a bath and a meal on a plate, sitting at a table, with cutlery and a waiter. How civilised.

We were very honoured at our last meal in the desert. The Sheikh of the tribe arrived with a freshly killed goat to be prepared and served in our honour and to say goodbye. This preparation and cooking time, took over four hours and it was nearly 10.30.p.m before it was ready to be eaten.

The animal must have been nearly 100 years old before being slaughtered. It was tough as old boots and full of gristle and fat. It was repulsive. None of us could eat it even though we were so hungry as we hadn't eaten for some eight hours. In the dark we carefully put all the bits of flesh into a rubbish bag, hoping that the Sheikh would not notice what we were doing. I am not sure what the punishment would be for offending a tribal elder, but luckily he never noticed, we hoped, what we did with the goat. I was looking forward to breakfast time. I think by now I could eat anything that didn't move. Well almost anything.

All our meals to this point had been very good, tasty and fulfilling. Meal times were always quite eventful as all the food is stuffed into a piece of unleavened bread and consumed with the fingers.

Our last morning arrived and breakfast of boiled eggs, falafel and tea were consumed very avidly. All night long my stomach had rumbled waiting for this feast. Breakfast over we packed our bags and they were loaded onto the four by four truck. We said our sad farewells to all the Bedouin with many a thank you and just a few tears.

The week had been an experience of life in the raw and I didn't want to leave it all behind me. Eventually that time came and the truck moved off slowly across the desert. We waved goodbye until we could no longer see our new found friends.

We now have to endure a very hot, bumpy ride across the desert. We were stuck in soft sand twice, but with help from all on board we made our escape, and suddenly there was a road ahead. It was impossible for the untrained eye to tell where the desert left off and the road began. How did our driver do it? One bit of desert to me looks the same as the next bit, but then I'm not a Bedouin.

We then had to endure another four hour ride in the truck. As you can imagine, air conditioning is not on the agenda. The heat was almost unbearable. To sit in a truck with 12 people, sweating profusely is something I will not try to describe, but I'm sure imagination could take over at this point.

Water was consumed at an alarming rate, which causes another problem, but I promise not to dwell on that. After crossing many borders protected by armed guards we finally, and with much relief, arrived at St. Katharine's Monastry.

Suddenly there were people everywhere. This was the most I had seen in seven days and I was not happy with the crowd. There were camels taking tourists up the hill to the Monastry, loads of stalls selling Bedouin memorabilia, small Arab boys trying their level best to sell me an alabaster egg. Why would I want one? I can buy them anywhere in England in Harrods or Dickens and Jones. I tried on several occasions to say an emphatic *no* to these small boys, but they followed me everywhere.

Finally I was told not to speak to them and don't look them in the eyes and then they will leave you alone and get the message. This worked I'm glad to say.

One of the ladies in our group happened to know one of the monks living in the monastry. He came from the same part of the world as her which was Devon. To not only see a monk in the monastry but to hear him speak with a very broad Devonian accent was remarkable to say the least. He then gave us a private tour of the monastry, visiting places that normal tourists were not allowed to see. We all felt very privileged and at least it was cooler inside than out.

Once the tour had finished we were ushered outside into a massive crowd of people all trying to touch the burning bush which eventually I managed.

The next out of character happening was the smell of cooking food, for the tourists. It didn't seem to fit in with the atmosphere of the monastry in the middle of the Sinai desert. In my opinion tourism and money had taken over this part of the desert.

Before leaving the area I went to see the foot hills of Mount Sinai and watch tourists starting their walk. They looked like ants. The mountain is enormous.

On walking back down the hill to our waiting truck and driver, I have to admit that I visited one of the stalls and bought myself a Kfir.

At last back in the truck we had to endure another four and a half hour ride to Sharm-el-Sheik and our Holiday Inn.

Here, we experienced a small technical problem; there had been a mix up with our bookings. The Hotels fault, not ours. The conclusion was that five of us had to share a room but with only three beds. After what we had all been used to in the desert we felt this was not a problem. So we were provided with mattresses and blankets and two of us kipped on the floor of this very large modern Hotel.

We all now needed to cool off, so we put on our swimming costumes and ran into the Red Sea. This was great. To feel water flowing all over the body was a luxury I had not felt for a whole week. I was sharing this bit of sea with a very large bright yellow and black angel fish that followed me wherever I went. It swam with me, between my legs and across my chest. I even managed to touch it and tickle his tail. I think it liked me and I was convinced this was due to my electric personality!

After a shower and wearing *clean* clothes we retired to the restaurant for a meal. It was served by a waiter, the food was on a plate and we ate with cutlery. It felt very strange. Once or twice I was nearly tempted to use my fingers again, but after a few glares from other restaurant users I finally declined and continued to use the knife and fork supplied.

By 8.30p.m we were ready for bed as we had to get up at 2.00.a.m to fly to Cairo then board another plane to Heathrow. We didn't know why the flights were altered, all we were told was that due to circumstances beyond their control these changes had to be made. I've learnt a good lesson, you don't argue with the authorities in Egypt.

The return flight home was uneventful and on time but we were stacked over Heathrow for thirty minutes before being allowed to land. I think it had something to do with the early hour of the morning.

I was now on English soil at last once more. Before everyone was allowed to disembark, the plane had to be fumigated. I had never experienced this before. It reminded me of the time many years ago when my sister and I contracted Scarlet Fever and the whole house had to be fumigated.

I'm sorry my age seems to be showing here, let's get back to the story.

There then developed another problem, the luggage took forty five minutes to appear. Whether a scorpion was found in my bags, I didn't know. No explanation as to why there was a hold up was ever given. I thought it might have had something to do with the fact that my luggage was in a bright orange survival bag held only together with two bungee straps.

Eventually, I arrived home tired, dirty and dusty, still covered in sand.

To live with the Bedouin, eat their type of food, share their desert, to have no toilet facilities, no water for washing, no tent, just put my bed roll down wherever it suits me is an experience I will never forget.

My knowledge on survival has remarkably improved and I now feel that I have some idea of how the other half live and more importantly, survive.

Sea sick in the Sinai I was not, even after eating very strange goat. I suffered no ill effects from their food at all. I would love to visit the desert again, now that I am more prepared for what could and did happen. The Bedouin are a very friendly group of people. We enjoyed their company, as they did ours.

Some of the money paid to the tour operator goes to each individual tribe to help with education and medical facilities. I felt this for me was a small price to pay for such a wonderful learning experience.

Two pieces of information that you all might like to share;

1.   Living in the desert is a very good way of losing weight. I don't want to brag, but I lost four pounds in seven days.
2.   Camels' droppings are very, very small and bear no relationship to the size of the animal.

I hope that everyone now feels that they know so much more about the desert.

Back at home in my kitchen I threw the survival bag on the floor and heaved a sigh of relief. I then went to the bathroom to enjoy for the first time for seven days what it was like to use a flushing toilet and then turn on a *tap* and not only wash my hands but dry them on a towel. This is civilisation. After a well deserved cup of English tea with milk, I decided to unpack my holdall.

I unhooked the bungee straps, but one of them got stuck underneath and would not release. So, without thinking clearly, I tugged at it. It became loose and at speed, it hit my eyebrow knocking me out and throwing me across the kitchen floor.

I came too at last covered in blood and with a swelling on my head the size of an egg which was growing with every minute that passed. Not only was I covered in blood but I was in some degree of pain, I felt sick and could not walk straight. I crawled to my front door as I saw my young neighbour come home from work and asked her for help. She took one look at me, uttered an expletive, took me back into my house, sat me down with a cloth over my wound and dialled 999.

Within less than five minutes I could hear the ambulance arriving with bells ringing and lights flashing. Not only an ambulance turned up but a Paramedic in a car. On entering my house, they examined me by taking my blood pressure and pulse also asking questions as to what exactly had happened. I was then placed in a wheelchair on oxygen and taken outside to the waiting ambulance.

The Doctor said that he didn't like the look of my injury. He was not alone, neither did I. With all lights flashing and bells ringing I arrived at the Accident and Emergency department of Epsom and General Hospital.

I was placed on a bed in a cubicle ready for examination. Finally a Doctor came to ask questions and ascertain exactly what had happened. I was then wheeled on a trolley to have my head examined.

I had not sustained a fracture and the cut only needed sterile strips to close the wound. I was told to take it easy for a few days as I had a mild concussion and a very bad headache. The examining Doctor did want to know why I was so dirty and covered in sand. I gave him a brief explanation and watched as his face registered utter surprise.

I telephoned my neighbour who kindly came to take me back home, help me unpack and cook my tea. She helped look after me for the next few days.

This trip taught me a valuable lesson:

The desert is not a dangerous place, but your kitchen back in civilisation most certainly is.

Whilst in Wyoming in the Bighorn Mountains I had the privilege of riding with an Apache Indian across the very spot where Custer had made his last stand.

You must now be "totally convinced" that I have always led a quiet life and that this will not be MY last stand.